Adopting Cats
and Kittens

Adopting is the most responsible option for anyone seeking a pet. Even the the most pathetic shelter cat or stray can usually blossom into a beauty such as this with the right kind and amount of care, love and patience.

Scott McKiernan

Adopting Cats and Kittens

A Care and Training Guide

Connie Jankowski

HOWELL BOOK HOUSE

New York

Maxwell Macmillan Canada
Toronto

Maxwell Macmillan International
New York   Oxford   Singapore   Sydney

Howell Book House
Macmillan Publishing Company
866 Third Avenue
New York, NY 10022

Maxwell Macmillan Canada, Inc.
1200 Eglinton Avenue East,
Suite 200
Don Mills, Ontario M3C 3N1

Macmillan Publishing Company is part of the Maxwell Communication Group of Companies.

Library of Congress Cataloging-in-Publication Data

Jankowski, Connie.
Adopting cats and kittens: a care and training guide / Connie
Jankowski.
    p. cm.
Includes bibliographical references
ISBN 0-87605-736-9
1. Cats. 2. Cats—Training. 3. Kittens. I. Title.
        SF447.J36   1993
    636.8—dc20   92-29844

Macmillan books are available at special discounts for bulk purchases for sales promotions, premiums, fund-raising, or educational use. For details, contact:

Special Sales Director
Macmillan Publishing Company
866 Third Avenue
New York, NY 10022

10 9 8 7 6 5 4 3 2 1

Printed in the United States of America

To the volunteers and shelter staffs who fight uphill battles to correct the errors of others.

To those who strive to educate the public—especially our youth—in hopes of bettering the lives of animals.

To veterinarians who provide low-cost spay and neuter programs.

To the millions of people who cherish their companion animals and appreciate the pleasures that only pets can provide.

And to Percy and Ryan, who always have time for a hug.

In spite of their reputation for aloofness and independence, cats are very social animals.

Nancy Klein

Contents

Foreword

by Roger Caras

FOUR THOUSAND years ago, in Egypt, man had a very exciting idea. A new invention—the silo—was introduced; it enabled man to plan for the production, storage and use of food. The silo inevitably attracted rodents, as pleased with the idea of grain storage as man was. The rodents themselves lured their own natural predators: snakes, ever-present birds of prey and the little, tough North African wildcats. The Egyptians now began to domesticate the wildcat. Domestication of dogs and goats had been going on, up to that point, for some fifteen thousand to twenty thousand years, having started several thousands of years earlier with the horse. Now it was the cat's turn. And with that development, a new idea in the history of human emotions was launched. A new kind of love was born!

The ancient Egyptians never did things by halves, however. In relatively short order, the cat they took in became a semigoddess, known as Basht or Bastet. An entire city was built in her honor, and orgies were even held on the Nile in specially designed boats to celebrate her rise to near-deity level. It was a strange mix of social progress, new technology and abnormal psychology. Only there and then it was not considered abnormal. The living cat itself was treated with enormous respect. To kill a cat in Egypt was regarded at that time as a capital crime. If a family's cat died, members of the household were expected to show all the customary signs of mourning for a specified period, including shaving their heads, rubbing themselves with ashes and slashing their clothes.

From Egypt, the cat spread to Europe and fared not quite as well as it had in the past. It became the familiar of witches, then virtually the devil himself. All kinds of lurid tales grew up, not just about black cats but about all cats. This vilification of the cat reached perhaps its highest level of idiocy in Elizabethan England when Queen Elizabeth I had a life-size model of the pope made of straw, had the container stuffed full of live cats, and then set it afire herself so that the screaming cats inside would make a mockery of the Catholic church. There are cases on record of cats being tried as criminals and publicly executed. It was a difficult time to be a cat.

In America today, we are apparently positioned somewhere between Elizabethan England and ancient Egypt in our attitude toward the cat. We do not burn cats to death in mad rituals, nor do we worship them—most of us, that is. We do, however, neglect cats, and that's almost as bad as the worst thing that ever happened to them. We live by a strange fiction that cats are able to care for themselves: that they don't need us, that they don't need veterinary care or proper nutrition, and that if we move and don't want to take our cats, it's fine to leave them behind to fend for themselves. All that is about as silly as you can get—but unfortunately, our cats suffer.

Such neglect and abandonment is, in fact, outright cruelty. The solution to this problem of neglect is to undertake the education of cat owners to spay and neuter their cats, coupled with realistic adoption of cats and kittens. Connie Jankowski, a genuinely sensible and well-informed author, gives us solid, down-to-earth advice on these matters in *Adopting Cats and Kittens*.

Realistic adoption involves screening of homes to make sure that the people accepting the animals can afford to care for them, want to care for them and know what they are doing. Unrealistic adoption is passing cats out of a cardboard box at the entrance to a shopping mall or in a parking lot anywhere. Kittens are terribly appealing, and they are frequently taken home on impulse, only to be abandoned or badly treated. It must not be!

Adopting an animal should never be an impulsive act or a reflexive response to a sweet face and a soft mew. Adoption can bring joy—or frustration, if such an adoption consumes discretionary funds or eats into a strained budget.

It is sad but true that a cat going to a poor home, an uncaring home, an uneducated home is better off with a quiet, merciful death. A badly placed animal moves from one home to the next, from one generation to the next, back and forth, until it is nearly wild with anxiety, uncertainty and insecurity. At that point, it is probably useless as a pet and will eventually be euthanized, if it is not killed by a car or a truck or disease. There are fates worse than death—and that is not just a cliché.

Because the cat has been in our care for only four thousand years or so, as compared with the much longer time in the case of dogs and goats and even horses, the cat's genetic potential has not really been exploited through selective breeding. Not yet. Dogs range in size from two pounds to well over two hundred pounds, whereas most cats range within a few pounds—that is, somewhere between six and seven pounds—of the norm. It is unusual for any cat to weigh even two or three times that much, whereas large dogs, depending on their breed, can regularly weigh two hundred times as much as the smallest dogs of another breed. It is important to remember that all cats, like all dogs, belong to one species, *Felis familiaris*. In the wild, however, cats vary enormously in size—from a ten-pound wildcat to the Siberian tiger of almost eight hundred pounds. It is entirely possible that the enormous flexibility of the cat family (Felidae) may someday be reflected within the species that we have taken into our homes.

The history of man and cat has really just begun. We have a very long road to travel together. It is critical that we in our relationship with this sensitive animal fully understand its needs, rejoice in its companionship and great beauty, and anticipate its future with excitement and wonder. The future, though, is the child of the present, and we owe it to all the cats now alive and to all cats that are yet to come to know what we are doing. This is a book to help us do just that.

Roger Caras is known and respected wherever there are people who care about animals and their well-being. A tireless champion of all animals, he is an eloquent spokesman for their humane treatment and informed care. Mr. Caras is justly renowned as a writer, commentator, ASPCA president and ambassador for those beings whose world we share and who enhance our very lives in so many ways.

Nancy Klein

Preface

CATS DEMAND little and give generous amounts of affection. A quiet evening at home becomes most enjoyable when a cat fills the silence with a purr, a glance or a nudge. Cats make great company. It's no wonder that the cat is the most popular companion animal in the United States. Nearly 60 million cats inhabit approximately 30 million households. What makes the cat so popular as a pet?

People enjoy cats. Their comical antics, their intense curiosity about their surroundings and the contented smile of a relaxed cat are cherished by those who know them. Each cat has a personality that can be discovered. A cat can add a dimension to a home; the presence of a cat simply brings a feeling that all is well with the world.

A house is not a home without a cat. I, like many animal lovers, have suffered the frustration of living in "no pet" housing. Too many apartment complexes deny renters the opportunity to enjoy the companionship of a cat or dog. When we moved from Pennsylvania to California we left behind friends and family. Feeling homesick and alone, I begged our apartment managers to let me have a cat. I offered a security deposit, and I offered to allow periodic inspections of our unit. My pleading was to no avail—pet ownership was denied on the basis of setting a precedent. After all, if I had a cat, everyone would soon want one. (Is that so bad?)

My husband and I worked many years to acquire the necessary down payment for our first house, and its purchase was a turning point in my life. The excitement of becoming homeowners reflected the reality that we could finally have pets. Our dog Misha was purchased before we moved into our new home, and a second dog, Trouble, was acquired during our first month of residence. A visit to Pennsylvania concluded with my collection of the family cat, Percy. The arrival of our dog Teddy preceded the birth of our son, Matt, who later wanted a pet of his own. Ryan, a beautiful black pantherlike kitten, was adopted from our local animal shelter to fulfill Matt's desires.

People are often surprised to learn that I have both cats and dogs. "How do they get along?" inquire puzzled acquaintances. Expecting to hear that the cats are kept separate from the dogs, many are surprised to learn of the special bonds that exist between my pets. Teddy and Percy are pals; they tease each other and play hard. Ryan looks upon Trouble (my male dog) as a surrogate mother. She kneads the thick mane of his Keeshond coat and sleeps curled in the warmth of his belly.

Our dogs and cats bring joy to our lives. Watching them coexist and share their joie-de-vivre is inspirational. Our family is closer because we enjoy the pets, and Matt is learning valuable lessons sharing in the care of our furry family members.

Pets are companions and therapists for their human friends. Pets are known to lower blood pressure, reduce stress and keep people on schedules. Exceptional pets have alerted their owners to fires, intruders and dangerous gases. I can't imagine being without pets. If you share my thoughts, a cat may be in your future.

Whether you adopt a cat from an animal shelter, off the street or from a volunteer humane group, you must make a commitment *before* you acquire a cat or kitten. Are you prepared to care for this cat for the duration of its life? Pets are not disposable; they become family members. Carefully examine your life-style, your finances and your future plans. If you measure up to the standards of a responsible pet owner, you are ready to reap the rewards of sharing your life with a feline friend.

Acknowledgments

THIS BOOK could not have been produced without the guidance of Seymour Weiss and Sean Frawley of Howell Book House. Their support and patience are greatly appreciated by this author.

Carol Lea Benjamin's *Second-Hand Dog* was the inspiration for this project. Carol's insights and her encouragement on this project are much appreciated.

Susan and John Hamil, D.V.M., are my friends and are examples of unselfish volunteers who serve animals. Their association with the Bluebell Foundation for Cats and John's review of the medical chapters in this book are invaluable.

Nancy Goodwin and Carl Pangano, directors of the Laguna Beach Animal Shelter and the Irvine Animal Care Center shared their insights and the professionalism of the best animal welfare workers.

The talents of Scott McKiernan and Nancy Klein have brought life to these pages via photographs and illustrations. It is obvious that Scott and Nancy's love of animals combines well with their artistic talents to capture the essence of their feline subjects. I know many readers will recognize their cats' qualities in the art.

Cat owners who have contributed photos and their success stories are the real stars of this book. May they inspire others to follow their lead.

Finally, I must thank my family, especially my husband, Stan, and son, Matt, for supporting me with this project.

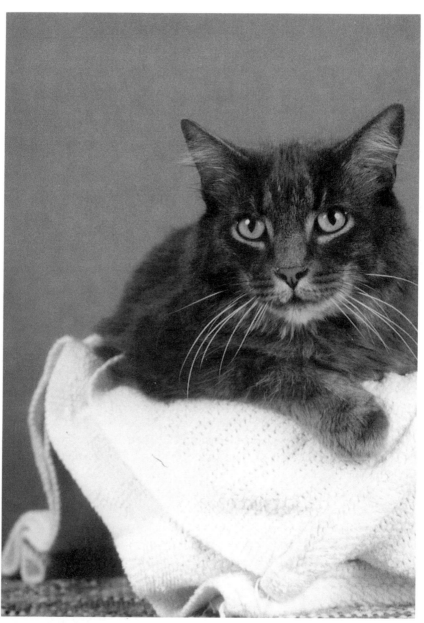

In every animal shelter there are potentially wonderful pet cats waiting for caring people to adopt them and give them new lives.   *Scott McKiernan*

1

The Shelter Cat

HOW DO CATS get to animal shelters? Some are strays; some are relinquished by their owners. Most are the result of unplanned litters. All animal shelters house potentially great pets waiting for adoption, but shelters differ in their funding and their operations. Budgets, space and personnel naturally restrict shelter operations.

CARING MAKES A DIFFERENCE

Shelters vary in size from huge, modern, metropolitan structures to small-town contracts to house strays in private kennels. Their daily operations differ according to the number of animals they receive and the support they get from their communities. Regardless of their mode of operation, shelters employ caring, devoted people who use their resources to assist needy animals. Many also rely heavily on volunteers.

A wonderful example of a small city shelter is in Laguna Beach, California. According to Nancy Goodwin, director of the shelter, cats are quarantined for their first ten days at the shelter, during which time owners have the opportunity to claim their lost cats. In contrast, the county shelter limits this holding time to seventy-two hours. Unfortunately, less than five percent of the cats are ever claimed by their owners.

Laguna cats are examined by a veterinarian and an animal behaviorist after the quarantine periods have passed. Not all shelters have outside professionals to perform these functions, but most shelters screen pets before they are offered for adoption. At Laguna, cats are flea bathed, wormed, vaccinated and spayed or neutered before they are ready for adoption. Kittens in Laguna are spayed or neutered when they are as young as eight weeks of age. Goodwin reports no adverse side effects to the early surgeries.

Shelters require potential adopters to complete applications as part of the screening process. As the applicants complete their paperwork, they can discuss with shelter personnel any questions they might have. In Laguna Beach a $45 fee (fees vary from shelter to shelter, but expect to pay a minimum of $25 to adopt a cat) is required with the application, which is less than it costs the shelter to process and feed the cats. Laguna will not release pets on the day the application is completed; the potential owners must wait at least twenty-four hours before claiming their new pets.

Animal shelters provide services that prevent needless suffering. Laguna Beach is an outstanding example of how a shelter can be run. Community education, vaccine clinics and spay/neuter programs complement the animal care at the shelter.

The Irvine (California) Animal Care Center is another model shelter. Among the services provided are pet rescue and animal adoptions, but Irvine's commitment to animals goes even further. Carl Pangano, director of the shelter, takes pride in its "Get Acquainted" room. Pangano recommends that potential adopters bring all family members (including pets) to the shelter to meet the pet to be adopted. This enables people to make good choices. Linda Greaves, an animal health technician who cares for the Irvine pets, encourages people to spend time with the cats before a selection is made.

Irvine employs a program specialist whose job it is to conduct educational programs. She visits every elementary school in the city at least once a year, while secondary schools receive occasional visits. Children in Irvine schools are instructed in the proper way to care for pets and how to become responsible pet owners. Occasionally, homeowners' associations or adult groups request similar presentations, and the shelter is happy to oblige.

Irvine benefits from an active community group that supports the shelter. P.A.W.S. holds fund-raising events to raise money for medical needs of the pets, shelter improvements and extended-stay fees for dogs and cats.

Pangano cites moving as the number-one reason for owners' relin-

Humane societies vary with the needs and size of the community. This is a view of the entryway to the Irvine (California) Animal Care Center, a model facility that offers a variety of programs and services area residents find beneficial.

The act of adopting requires that certain information be provided to help pair a potential adopter with the right animal. Here at Irvine the paperwork is being completed to facilitate the perfect match.

quish their pets. This emphasizes the need for stability *before* a pet is brought into a home. Pet owners should make every effort to take their pets with them when they move. Unfortunately many people think first of their own convenience, not taking their pets' love and devotion into account.

Pangano emphasizes that adoptions should be "for the life of the pet." People should consider all the expenses of pet ownership *before* they take home a pet. Adoption fees are but a small part of the cost of owning a pet. Food, supplies, veterinary fees, grooming, pest control and boarding will require expenditures of cash throughout the pet's life.

The Irvine shelter is seeing a decrease in the number of puppies brought in, while continuing to receive lots of kittens. Pangano says the biggest challenge to a shelter is dealing with the sheer volume of pets. May through October is the busiest time for kitten activity. Health problems of roaming cats also challenge control.

Goodwin and Pangano acknowledge their communities' support, saying the shelters could not exist without the volunteer work force. Donations of supplies and funds also help the staff to care for the needy animals. Perhaps you can support a shelter in your area; you will find volunteer work to have many rewards.

The goal of every shelter is to be needed less. Responsible pet ownership is the key to overcoming the problem of pet overpopulation. Perhaps one day shelters will achieve their goals and then be able to dedicate their resources to other animal-related projects.

SAFE HAVEN (The Bluebell Foundation for Cats)

In addition to government shelters, there are numerous cat-rescue organizations across the country. These organizations are privately funded and depend upon donations of funds, personnel (volunteers) and supplies.

Before patronizing such an organization, carefully check its reputation. Your veterinarian, the humane society or a friend may be able to provide a reference for the integrity of a local privately run cat assistance group.

Does the group house cats in a shelterlike environment, or are cats kept in foster homes until they are adopted? Do the cats receive veterinary care prior to adoption? Are they spayed or neutered? Can personnel provide temperament evaluations?

The Bluebell Foundation for Cats in Laguna Beach, California, was founded by the late Bertha Yergat, a lover of cats. She willed a two-acre

4

The Bluebell Foundation for Cats is a haven for homeless felines. A house was converted to accommodate the needs of more than one hundred feline guests.

Even the sign at Bluebell proclaims welcome.

A cream-colored calico nuzzles a photo of Bertha Yergat, founder of Bluebell.

home and a million dollars to establish a protection society for her feline friends. The foundation is administered by a board of directors who manage the facility by hiring personnel, handling finances, providing for veterinary care, managing the facilities and establishing policies.

The facility houses approximately 150 cats who enjoy a ''no time limit'' stay at the cat colony. Some of the cats were strays, a few were once abused, but many of the cats were ''willed'' to Bluebell's care. Such cats come with endowments, or pensions, provided by their previous owners to cover expenses throughout the life of the cat.

The resident care-provider knows the cats by name (each cat wears a heart-shaped identification tag to help visitors to know TJ from Emily, for instance) and can give each cat's health and behavior history.

Although many of the cats will be lifetime residents at Bluebell, cats are available for adoption to the right homes. The cats can go only to places that will be at least as good for the cat as Bluebell. Whether fluffy or sleek, outgoing or reserved, each cat is an individual. Potential cat adopters are treated to the opportunity to visit the cats and discover their personalities before making an adoption. Each cat receives veterinary clearance and is spayed or neutered before leaving the facility.

Running such an establishment is no small feat. Monthly expenditures often exceed $6,000, and financial contributions offset rising costs of food, cat litter, medications, pesticides and operations. Donations of housewares (pillows, blankets, carpet, furniture, towels and cleaning products), cat supplies (scratching posts, litter boxes, bedding, toys and feeding dishes) and labor (cat cuddlers and maintenance workers) enable the facility to stay afloat.

Credit for keeping this wonderful establishment operating belongs to the foundation's board of directors. Philip May, a longtime humane activist, heads the board. Kay Cox, head of a regional occupational training program for veterinary assistants, helps recruit volunteers. Dorothy Palmer (whose garage typically houses ten to fifteen rescue cats) is the financial brain of the board. All cat lovers, these caring people donate their talents and time to Bluebell.

Completing the board, John and Susan Hamil contribute their time and expertise to meet the medical needs of the cats. John, a veterinarian, and Susan, an accredited animal health technician, see that the cats receive vaccinations, treatment for parasites and other medical care as necessary. These caring individuals provide these services because they believe Yergat's dream of providing for needy cats is worthwhile. That dream is the adhesive that holds the group together.

While Bluebell is a California-based foundation, other cat foundations exist in the United States. Most groups would envy the resources of the Bluebell Foundation, but they share in the dedication to saving cats from human neglect.

Consider supporting a humane organization in your area—whether government run or privately run. They will appreciate your time or your donations. They will certainly be happy to accept financial contributions (some are tax-deductible). When you make such a contribution, both you and the cats will benefit. You're sure to feel good about helping our companion cats.

An Amazing Bluebell Story

Cats who reside at Bluebell aren't just charges, they are individuals, and each is appreciated for its special qualities. When cats are adopted out, the departures from the facility are bittersweet. Going to a caring family is a wonderful opportunity for a cat, and the Bluebell staff is happy to see the cats begin their new lives. However, staff members become attached to the cats, and saying good-bye is sometimes difficult.

Bluebell cats leave with an invitation to return at any time. If the cat doesn't adjust to its family members or their other pets, if the new cat owner becomes ill or cannot support the cat, the cat must be returned to Bluebell.

One special cat, Lacey, temporarily resided at Bluebell. Eventually, the cat's previous owner reclaimed the cat and moved to northern California with a friend. Tragically, the cat owner was found murdered a few months later, and the Bluebell people immediately searched for the cat.

It is assumed that the cat witnessed the violent crime and escaped from the scene. Searches for the cat in the vicinity of the crime were in vain. No strays or local shelter cats fit Lacey's description. Hope for recovering the cat diminished as time passed.

One day a vocal cat was heard outside the Bluebell doors. Investigation produced joy and awe. Waiting to be readmitted to Bluebell was Lacey, wearing the same identification tag she had when she left!

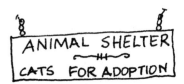

If you know the type of cat you want before going to the shelter, the selection of your special pet will be made much easier.

Nancy Klein

2

Choosing a Cat
for Adoption

WHAT SHOULD YOU LOOK FOR in a cat? Of the thousands available for adoption, how will you select one from among the fabulous feline faces? Before you start looking, think about the characteristics you like in a cat. Consider:

- Personality. A cat that approaches you and makes eye contact is usually a good bet. A friendly, outgoing personality is desired by most pet owners, but some people prefer a cat that is less demanding.
- Age. Although kittens are adorable, they can be a handful. Kittens are active and require some training. Many people prefer to adopt mature cats that are trained and relaxed.
- Breed or Type. If you don't like to groom, don't get a long-haired cat. All cats need grooming, but longhairs require extra brushing.
- Healthy. Everyone wants a cat that is fit, but don't overlook the cat that has recovered from an illness. Often the care the cat is given to combat the illness makes the cat stronger in the long run, and the handling during treatment can make the cat easier to handle at home.

Shelter personnel are trained to evaluate animals; consult them for their opinions of the cats they have on hand. Sometimes it is best just to wait for the right cat to come along.

The age of technology has arrived to serve the field of animal welfare. Cat adoptions have been completed via the airwaves, facilitated by television. Our cable network in California airs a terrific program, *The Pet Place*, which features cats and dogs from local animal shelters. This opportunity to display available cats and dogs has enabled our shelters to place hundreds of needy animals in wonderful homes.

Our local ABC affiliate occasionally features adoptable pets. Local talk-shows are natural ways to showcase the wonderful animals waiting for homes to call their own. In addition to servicing the lucky, featured pets, these shows provide a bigger service—they call attention to the need for responsible pet ownership.

Seeing homeless cats should be an incentive for spaying and neutering the Fluffies and Pumpkins of our neighborhoods. We depend upon this mainstream media coverage of pet issues to improve the future for all animals. Of course, the best message heard from the broadcasts is that wonderful animals need homes, and the shelter is the place to look for a cute cat.

BEFORE YOU LEAP

Your local animal shelter can open the door to future happiness. Your enthusiasm for becoming a pet owner may make you impatient, but before you head for the nearest humane society, carefully examine your decision.

Although cats are fabulous, you *must* be prepared to meet their basic needs. The fact that you love cats—no matter how much—is not enough. The goal of adopting a cat is to provide the cat with a *permanent* home. Think before you move—and be prepared.

Never surprise a friend with the gift of a pet. Even people who fawn over kittens, who declare they want a cat just like yours and who read pet care books from cover to cover, may not be prepared for the responsibility of pet ownership. If you are considering participating in the selection of a friend's pet, be sure he or she welcomes the responsibility and is prepared to meet the pet's needs.

Shelter volunteers are vital to the continued functioning of many institutions.

Living Arrangements

It is unfair to cats to place them in housing where they are unwanted or not allowed. Sneaking a cat into an apartment can backfire. Even if you confine the cat to the indoors, it is sure to make its presence known.

Cats are drawn to sunshine. Your "secret" is likely to discover that your windows are a source of light and perch on the windowsill. The activity on the other side of the glass will enchant your cat, enticing it to observe the falling leaves, singing birds and other cats passing by.

Landlords are likely to show up at the worst possible times. A leaky faucet, a broken dishwasher or the neighbors' complaints about noise or bugs results in a knock at the door and a curious superintendent's entry. Your cat will be out of the bag!

People who move frequently, such as students, military personnel and corporate trainees should consider waiting until they settle into a home before they get a cat. Those who are really determined to succeed, however, can usually find places that will accept pets. These places are sometimes hard to find, less convenient than other living choices and involve increased expenses—security deposits and/or higher rents.

Many people (no matter how ingenious they are in attempting to hide their pets) meet with utter disappointment when their smuggled pets are discovered.

Time Factor

Cats need your companionship as much as you want theirs. Will you have time to spend with your cat? Busy work schedules, vacations and time at outside interests keep us from our homes. Although cats are somewhat independent, they do need companionship.

Cats don't care if their human companions are young or old, rich or poor, as long as their basic needs are met. Family members, roommates and other pets can supplement the time you spend with your cat, but busy schedule or not, having a pet is a commitment to spending time with it.

Expenses

The initial expenses of acquiring a cat include adoption fees, veterinary fees (inoculations, worming, spaying or neutering) and purchase of supplies. Your cat will need a high-quality cat food, and cat litter will appear on your weekly shopping list. Annually your cat will need to visit the veterinarian for booster shots, worming and a general examination.

You must be prepared to spend sufficient time with your cat to build and sustain a happy relationship. A little face-to-face nuzzling is never lost on an appreciative feline friend and often secures the bond between you.

Animals in multicat households can enjoy the good company of both feline and human companions.

Occasionally you will confront unexpected expenses. Veterinary emergencies, flea control, grooming and boarding require expenditures beyond the normal budget. You must be prepared to meet all your cat's normal and special needs.

FINDING YOUR CAT

Public animal shelters take in many thousands of cats each year. These cats depend upon adoption to save them from euthanasia. Shelters offer a variety of wonderful cats. Whether your preference is a fluffy longhair or a sultry shorthair, you're sure to find the cat of your dreams at the shelter—then you'll wonder how anyone could have deserted these marvelous pets!

Animal shelters employ experts to service their charges. These amazing people not only care deeply about the welfare of cats and dogs; they are also skilled in many disciplines. Shelter personnel are experts in handling pets; most can accurately assess the temperaments of the cats and help to match the cats with suitable owners.

Most shelters provide medical care for their cats. Veterinarians, many of whom are volunteers, examine cats and dogs, treat existing illnesses and provide preventive medicine. These procedures screen the cats for adoption and ensure that they are free of contagious diseases.

A conscientious shelter worker will get to know you before releasing a pet to your charge. Be prepared to discuss your life-style, living arrangements and means for supporting a pet. When you are ''interrogated,'' answer honestly, and don't be offended. The animal control officer is trying to help you make a good decision and to place the cat in a permanent home.

Private rescue groups supplement the work of animal shelters in many areas of this country. Foundations are often established to support the work of caring volunteers. These groups often take in strays and rescue animals from unfortunate home situations. Private donations, trusts and grants support the work of these rescue organizations. Most groups have limitations of funding and housing and are happy to place their charges in the hands of suitable new owners.

Medical standards differ among private rescue groups. Some are associated with veterinarians who provide health care; others leave this responsibility to the prospective owners. Be sure to inquire about health records and take copies to your veterinarian on your first visit.

These groups vary, however, in their expertise in handling and placing pets. Furthermore, the charters of these organizations differ in provisions for disposing of unwanted animals. Before contributing to these groups check out their policies. Avoid any organization that allows cats or dogs to be used for laboratory research, or one that doesn't screen potential owners.

Strays that wander the streets can make wonderful pets; or others can be emotional and physical wrecks. Depending upon the condition of the individual cat, you may or may not be prepared to rehabilitate and care for a stray.

Strays come without benefit of health certificates. So before exposing existing pets to a stray, take the cat to your veterinarian for a thorough examination. If you decide to keep a stray, vaccinate it on the same schedule you would follow for a kitten.

Some strays will walk into your home and fit right in. Others may resent captivity and fight for freedom. These special cats need owners with patience, understanding of feline behavior and realistic expectations. There is great satisfaction in taming a stray cat and seeing it blossom into a contented pet. However, if the situation gets out of control, consult your local animal shelter for advice or assistance.

For a happy welcome to your home, plan ahead and have everything in readiness for your new cat's arrival.

3

Preparing for Kitty's Arrival

IN ORDER to assure a smooth transition for your new cat and your family, plan ahead for Kitty's arrival. Avoid the last-minute scurry to gather supplies and make decisions about caring for your new pet. You will need a cat carrier to transport your new pet home, and the home must also be prepared before the cat's arrival.

WELCOMING YOUR NEW CAT

A cat adopted from a shelter has been living in stressful conditions. Confinement, close proximity to strange people and animals, and noise can easily stress a cat. To help your new pet adapt to your household, try to keep its first days in the home stress-free.

Allow the cat to explore its new home. Show the cat its litter box. Introduce pets and people gradually. Supervise the cat's activities, and confine it when your attention is needed elsewhere.

Don't expect the cat to instantly adapt to your household routine. Expect the cat to hide under the bed or behind the couch for a few days. This gives the cat the opportunity to observe your actions and build trust in you. When the cat is secure and comfortable, it will participate in the activities of the household.

Shelter adoptees can be devoted companions for many years. But they may need special consideration during the first few weeks. If you have any questions or problems, contact your local animal shelter for advice.

Preparing Your Pets

Incorporating a new pet into a family that already has pets is usually easy, but occasionally a newcomer presents a challenge. This meshing of old with new requires patience and planning. Before acquiring a new cat or kitten, evaluate the feline, canine, avian and any other pets in your home.

Make notes on each pet, assessing the temperament of each. Is Fluffy or Scruffy likely to openly accept the new cat, act indifferent or be outwardly aggressive to the newcomer? Identify potential problems.

Spend extra time interacting with existing pets before the new cat comes to live with you. Grooming a resident cat, or practicing obedience exercises with a dog, will help to reinforce your dominance, while it boosts the confidence of the pet at hand. Added attention will help create a feeling of security for your pets, so that the arrival of the new family member will be less threatening to your established pets.

Facing the Family

Whether your household includes members of several generations or just you, all members of your family must come to agreement about the niceties and annoyances of a feline addition. Family members often have differing opinions about life—why should cat ownership be any different? Prior to the arrival of a new pet, your family should call a meeting to discuss the fine points of pet ownership. (If you are a family of one, have a frank discussion with yourself.)

Often people think that it would be great to have a pet. But the mental image of life with that pet is different for each person expressing the idea. Your family meeting should include discussion of the following:

- Where will the cat sleep?
- What will the cat eat?
- Will the cat be permitted outdoors?
- Who will be responsible for feeding the cat?

"Mighty" is the much-loved pet of ten-year-old Sarah Girard—a kitten with a *mighty* bright future from the look of things.

Have a secure carrier ready to bring your cat home for the first time. Later the carrier will be indispensable for vet visits and other trips away from home.   *Nancy Klein*

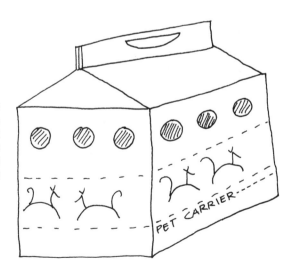

- Who will purchase cat food and supplies?
- Who will be responsible for obtaining veterinary care?

Prior to the arrival of your feline family member, discuss the cat's needs with your family. Although an adult must assume primary responsibility for the care of any pet, children can be responsible for specific daily tasks.

Establish a schedule for routine tasks such as feeding, grooming and changing the litter box. Determine the time, place and person to be responsible for each task. Special needs such as bathing, nail trimming and making veterinary appointments must be looked after for your cat's well-being and should be the responsibility of an adult.

If anyone in the household suffers from allergies, special precautions should be taken. Is this person allergic to cats specifically? How severe are the allergies? An allergist (M.D.) should be consulted *before* any pets are brought into the house. Can medication be prescribed to reduce allergic reactions?

If the person can tolerate being around a cat, it may be possible to proceed with plans to acquire a new pet if you follow the following suggestions: the allergic person should not groom the cat, sleep with the cat, or allow the cat to lick his or her skin. Follow the doctor's advice regarding medication and desensitization techniques. Try applying products such as Allerpet (available through pet-supply outlets) to the cat's coat. This will help control dander.

Groom your cat regularly—especially during shedding season—to avoid a buildup of hair in the house. In severe cases, such as with asthmatics, it may not be practical to have a cat in the home.

FOOD REQUIREMENTS

What is the best diet for your pet cat? Cats like tuna, milk and meat scraps from your plate. Feeding cats "people food" not only develops finicky eaters, but is also not healthy for cats.

Commercial cat foods are formulated based on the results of scientific studies. Pet-food companies invest time and money to study nutritional needs of cats and dogs. These data are used in formulating balanced nutritious foods to meet these needs.

Special foods are currently available for cats throughout their life cycles. Kitten products are made to meet the needs of the growing cat and should be fed to cats throughout the first year of life, even though

There is a great variety of types of cat food readily available. Ask your veterinarian about
the kind and amount of food you should be giving your cat.
Nancy Klein

the cat may appear "full grown" at about six months of age. Cats, like people, mature at different rates, and your veterinarian should examine the cat when it is one year old. At that time the vet may recommend continuing the kitten food or suggest switching to a maintenance food.

Read the Labels

Cat foods vary in price, appearance, packaging and, of course, ingredients. Don't be lured by the attractive box or drastically low prices of some pet foods. A cute picture doesn't assure that the food in the can or box is right for your cat. Generic or store-brand foods often lack vital nutrients and can harm your pet over time. Discuss pet-food selection with your veterinarian to ensure that your cat is properly fed.

Treats

Commercial treats for cats are widely available in grocery and pet stores. Although these treats are made especially for cats, they are not intended to be complete diets. Remember to watch your cat's bowl and to monitor its feeding habits. If your cat eats significantly less than the portion recommended on the cat-food label, try cutting back on treats. If the problem persists, or if your cat appears to be losing weight, discuss the matter with your veterinarian.

Household treats should be limited to foods that are good for cats. An occasional tidbit from the fridge or a saucer of milk won't ruin your cat's health, but such treats don't meet your cat's nutritional needs. The bulk of your cat's diet should come from a high-quality cat food.

YOUR CAT'S NEEDS LIST

Cat food
Food and water bowls
Cat litter
Litter box liners
Scratching post
Kitty toys
Bedding
Flea-control products (if needed)
Cat shampoo
Cat brush

Cat comb
Nail clippers
Cotton swabs
Medical supplies (if recommended by a veterinarian or shelter worker)
Medical manual
Harness and leash
Pet carrier
Cat treats
Catnip

EMERGENCY PREPAREDNESS

Everyone shares in the responsibility to be prepared for any disaster. Be sure your emergency plans have incorporated your pet's needs. If you live in an area that is prone to earthquakes, hurricanes or fires, you should always be prepared to evacuate. Emergency personnel will be too busy tending to humans to respond to your cats' needs, so you must be able to protect them. Start by following these basic tips:

1. Make sure your cats wear current identification tags, including the phone number of a friend or relative who lives outside your geographic area.
2. Keep your cats' health records in a handy location.
3. Keep the name, telephone number and address of your cats' veterinarian available along with all medical records.
4. Authorize a neighbor to care for your cats in your absence. Written authorization is a must should your cats require veterinary care.
5. Be prepared by storing a seventy-two-hour supply of food and water for your cats and pet carriers with your cats' emergency kit. Be sure all medications your cats require are in the emergency kit.
6. Know the locations of animal shelters in your area.
7. Red Cross shelters will not allow pets inside their buildings. However, crated pets can be left outside the shelters, if you attend to them. Alternate temporary housing for your cats is ideal.
8. Contact your local Red Cross for information regarding emergency preparedness in your area.

For your cat's protection, keep a collar with identification tags attached to it on your pet at all times.

Children should be encouraged to partici- pate in the pet-owning experience, but an adult family member should establish guidelines and watch for the safety of the cat and the youngster.

KIDS AND CATS

I acquired my first cat, a black-and-white darling, when I was five years old. I found Fluffy outside our house, in the bushes. Although my parents hadn't planned on getting me a cat, neither had the heart to dispose of my new friend. Although the cat was "mine," it was my parents who accepted responsibility for the cat's needs.

Children often beg for pets, and doting parents give in. Although kittens are cute and fluffy, they grow into cats that will need care for many years. Unless the parents are willing to assume responsibility for a cat, the child might be better matched with a stuffed toy.

For the lucky children who are blessed with a childhood that includes pets, many pleasurable experiences can be derived from the relationship between child and pet. Children are comforted by the affections of a pet. Even when parents are too busy to give their children attention, the pets are always ready for loving. This bonding has a soothing effect, which helps build a child's self-image and self-confidence.

Children should be taught that cats are not to be mishandled in rough play. Cats need quiet time, and children should respect this need. Small children such as toddlers and babies should not be left alone with a cat without adult supervision.

Children can learn the importance of caring for another being when age-appropriate tasks are assigned to them. Feeding, litter box maintenance and grooming tasks can be made part of a child's chores, but don't expect a five-year-old to assume complete responsibility for his or her cat.

Older children can incorporate the family pet into lessons in budgeting, biology, writing and reading. Books and magazines about cats often convert reluctant readers by seducing them with a favorite subject.

Special times can be shared between pets and children; don't you have cherished childhood memories that include a treasured cat?

In an amazing variety of ways, your veterinarian is your partner in pet care.

Nancy Klein

4

Visiting the
Veterinarian

HAPPILY, cats today are living longer than ever before. Observant owners, good nutrition, the trend to confine cats to the indoors and advances in vaccines and veterinary care contribute to the extended life expectancy of the cat. Many cats are reaching their twenties, and the responsible cat owner can take pride in this advancement. Your veterinarian is your partner in pet care. Regular visits for immunizations, wormings, teeth cleaning and examinations are vital to the health of your precious kitty.

Cats differ from other mammals in the way they react to illnesses. Cats will not "tell" you when they are ill. While other pets, such as dogs, may openly display signs of illness, cats will hide their symptoms. This unusual behavior reflects a wild cat's survival instinct. To avoid conflicts with stronger animals, sick cats will hide until they recover from illness or die. Because domestic cats still hide illness, the cat owner's observation of his pets is crucial to their health.

Perhaps the only signal that a cat is ill will be the cat's retreat from its usual activities. If a cat hides from its family, appears to have decreased activity, exhibits a decrease in appetite, grooms itself continuously, or if the eyes have a different look to them, it may be harboring illness. The alert cat owner should immediately consult a veterinarian and schedule a physical examination.

THE VETERINARY EXAMINATION

Every newly adopted cat should be examined by a veterinarian. A wise person will schedule an appointment with the veterinarian on the same day that the cat is picked up. The veterinarian can examine the cat, and can answer any cat-care questions the new owner may have.

If you have other pets in your household, it is especially important to have your new cat examined before you bring it home. You certainly wouldn't want to endanger your other pets by bringing home a new pet that could be carrying a contagious disease.

The veterinarian can recommend a diet for your cat, based upon its age, health and weight. As discussed earlier in the section on food requirements, there are many commercial foods available. As ads for special cat foods proliferate, veterinarians are receiving more and more questions about feline diets. This signifies that cat owners are becoming aware of their cats' special needs. Attention to its proper diet will result in a longer life for your cat.

Your veterinarian should be able to advise you about any behavior problems or recommend an animal behaviorist to help you. Cat-care products are often recommended by veterinarians, and the doctor's advice can help you make wise purchases.

Cats, like all mammals, are complex organisms and subject to numerous health problems. However, routine preventive care can greatly increase the likelihood that a cat will reach old age. The diseases mentioned in this chapter are but a few examples of diseases that a cat can contract. Of course, every cat is an individual and therefore is a product of its individual genetic makeup, but the care it receives will affect its health.

Your veterinarian should monitor your cat's physical development from kittenhood through the golden years. By working as a team you and the doctor will give your cat its best chance for a long and healthy life. The *Cat Owner's Home Veterinary Handbook*, by Delbert G. Carlson, D.V.M., and James M. Giffin, M.D. (New York: Howell Book House, 1983), is a valuable resource for cat owners. This book describes in detail physical qualities of the cat and presents a detailed health picture. From emergency care to immunizations, this book provides a wonderful supplement to your veterinarian's advice.

An annual physical checkup is your cat's best health safeguard. Prevention is vital to your cat's well-being along with your alertness to any change in your cat's activity level or over-all condition.
Scott McKiernan

IMMUNIZATIONS

Your cat may be spared the tragedy of serious illnesses—if you practice preventive medicine and have it vaccinated against common cat diseases. All cats should be vaccinated, but cats that spend any time outdoors depend on diligent adherence to vaccination schedules.

Feline AIDS (FIV) can present a wide variety of symptoms, including what owners have described as "He just doesn't seem to feel well." It is thought that aggression among cats—particularly biting—is the most common route of passage of this disease. Therefore, the most likely victims are roaming, sexually intact cats. Fevers of 103° F or higher often develop from FIV infection, as do loss of appetite, infections of the mouth, skin problems, bladder problems, diarrhea and breathing difficulties. Occasionally seizures, disorientation and neurologic disorders appear. Treatment is symptomatic, although treatment of FIV itself is experimental. There is no vaccination; prevention requires isolating healthy cats from those that are infected. It must be noted that FIV differs significantly from human AIDS.

Feline Infectious Peritonitis (FIP) is spread from cat to cat and is a deadly disease. Occasionally an affected cat will exhibit depression, anorexia, weight loss and/or fever; however, many affected cats appear normal. One sign of FIP is swelling of the abdomen, which is caused by fluid retention. Eventually the fluid causes respiratory distress, which may be accompanied by jaundice or anemia. Abnormalities in the gastrointestinal system, the nervous system or the cat's vision may appear. Most affected cats survive no longer than two to three months, so vaccination is critical in preventing such a tragedy.

Rabies is transmitted through the saliva of affected animals via bites. This ancient disease can be transmitted by wildlife (including skunks, bats and raccoons) as well as domestic pets. Humans can also be affected. Rabies has two stages: furious and paralytic. During the furious stage, animals appear aggressive and uncontrollable. Rabid animals often snap, bite, chew and drool. The paralytic stage brings loss of bodily functions. Animals diagnosed as rabid should be humanely euthanized.

A very effective vaccine is available to prevent rabies. Most communities require dogs to be vaccinated for rabies before they can be licensed. However, some cat owners are lax in obtaining protection for their pets.

Be sure your vet inoculates your cat for rabies—especially if your cat is exposed to other animals.

Feline Enteric Coronavirus can cause vomiting and diarrhea. Symptoms are usually mild and chance of recovery is good. Unfortunately, there is no vaccination for this disease at this time.

Feline Panleukopenia Virus (often called cat fever) causes inflammation of the intestine, which then causes vomiting and diarrhea. Cells throughout the body are affected, and the number of white cells in the blood is drastically reduced. The disease is potentially fatal. Luckily, an effective vaccine for this disease is readily available.

Feline Leukemia Virus (FeLV), which is caused by a retrovirus, suppresses the cat's immune system. This condition can cause a variety of problems because the cat is generally weakened due to disease and infections. Poor wound healing, cancers, anemias, patches of tough skin and recurrent abscesses can often be attributed to the underlying condition known as FeLV. Vaccination for this condition is critical in maintaining the overall health of a cat, particularly for cats that go outdoors.

Rotavirus is a newly identified disease. This common disease usually produces mild or no symptoms in adult cats, but kittens are more drastically affected. Veterinarians can detect this disease by examining fecal specimens. Currently there is no vaccination for rotavirus.

Feline Viral Rhinotracheitis (FVR) is also known as feline herpesvirus. This disease usually involves lesions of the skin, eyes and/or mouth. Stress often precipitates an eruption of lesions.

Feline Calicivirus Infection (FCV) is an acute infection of the respiratory system. Similar in appearance to the human cold, FCV has many strains. Vaccinations are available, and multicat households should be especially careful to keep their cats current on this protection.

Feline Urinary Syndrome (FUS) occurs in both sexes when small crystals form in the bladder and make urination painful and difficult for the cat. Usually females (due to a wider urethra) can expel crystals but males often cannot. With urethral obstruction, urine backs up, eventually causing kidney failure. Perineal urethrostomy (surgery to enlarge the urethral opening) brings relief to affected cats who cannot be successfully managed medically. Treating FUS involves making passage of crystals possible; it does not eliminate crystal production, therefore dietary changes are important in preventing recurrence.

PARASITE CONTROL

Most cats encounter parasite infestation within their lifetimes. Depending upon the parasite, duration and severity of infestation damage range from negligible to life-threatening. You can protect your cat from parasites with good sanitation, regular grooming and microscopic examination of the cat's feces for eggs. Your veterinarian can identify and treat parasites your cat may acquire, including those listed here.

External Parasites

Flea control is one of the biggest challenges to pet owners. Summer is the season in which fleas seem to flourish, but warm climates provide an atmosphere that allows fleas to thrive throughout the year.

Fleas are irritating, and the constant itching and biting at fleas is obviously tiresome to your cat. Fleas are quickly spread to all pets in the household, and even people are bothered by the biting beasts. Fleas are more than a nuisance. They transmit tapeworms, which can infect your cat. They can also be the cause of serious illness, including anemia, which can threaten a cat's life, particularly if the cat is very young or very old.

Pet owners should observe their cats and dogs and take steps to eliminate fleas at the first signs of infestation. In order to eliminate fleas from your environment, you must treat your pets, your home and your yard on the same day. Fleas spend most of their time off the cat in the carpet and/or in the grass, only occasionally visiting your pets for a meal of blood. Unless you eliminate fleas from the home, yard and pet, they will quickly return.

To eliminate fleas take the three-step approach:

1. Bathe or dip the pets in your house. You might want to use the services of a professional groomer.
2. Flea-bomb your house or hire a professional exterminator to treat your house.
3. Spray your yard with pesticides or use an exterminator. Be careful in following the directions as the products are dangerous to you and your pets if used improperly.

Check your cat regularly for the presence of external parasites. Scratching is often a sign of flea infestation.

Part of any routine home exam should include a check of the ears. They should be cleaned gently on a regular basis and any dark wax or other foreign material brought to the attention of your veterinarian.

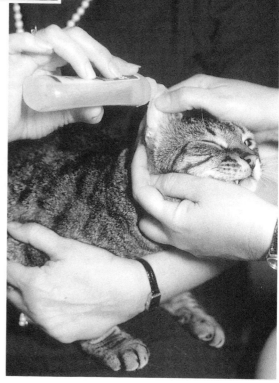

It is critical that the cat owner read the labels on flea-control products. Dips, shampoos, sprays and powders that are safe for dogs can be lethal when used on cats. Be sure the products you choose for your cats specify that they are intended for use on cats—and strictly follow the directions on the product label.

Ticks vary in significance throughout the country. Climate and geography dictate the species of ticks you may encounter, and therefore dictate the degree of threat they pose to you and your pets. Consult your veterinarian or local department of agriculture to determine the threat of ticks in your area. Indoor cats have very little chance for contact with ticks.

Ear Mites are microscopic arachnids that are commonly found on cats. An infected cat will often shake its head or scratch its ears with its back feet in an effort to relieve the itch created by the mites. Other signs of ear mites include rubbing the head on the floor or shaking it.

Ear mites often are accompanied by a gritty, black, waxy substance in the ear. The grit must be removed from the ear with cotton swabs, and medication must be put in the ear regularly to eliminate the parasites. Over-the-counter ear mite medications are available, but your best course of action is to consult your veterinarian for advice and treatment.

Ear mites can cause infection, loss of hearing, and equilibrium problems. Left untreated, ear mite infections can become very serious and even life-threatening.

Demodectic Mange is caused by mites (genus *Demodex*). Thinning hair, formation of pus-filled sores, and crusty, scaly skin characterize demodectic mange. Treatment for this condition requires the outer layer of skin to be peeled off using topical keratolytic agents. Antibacterial ointments and mite-killing potions are then applied to affected areas. Treatments continue for three to four weeks, until the skin scrapings are negative.

Lice are occasionally seen on cats, but are usually associated with neglect and unsanitary living conditions. Clinical signs include dry, scaly skin, which may or may not itch. Topical application of dips, shampoos or powders designed to kill lice will relieve the problem. Thorough cleaning of the cat's bedding and environment is needed to totally end the problem. Repeat the process once a week for four weeks. People and other pets in the household should be examined and, if necessary, treated for lice.

Internal Parasites

Parasites in the cat's gastrointestinal region can cause vomiting, diarrhea, anemia, dehydration and general failing health in a cat. Parasites can rob a cat of nutrients and weaken the cat's immune system. Many kinds of parasites threaten your cat's well-being, and many infestations display similar symptoms. Your veterinarian will be able to identify parasites and prescribe treatment. Among the more common parasites found in cats are the following:

Toxoplasma Gondii is the most common protozoan found in cats. This organism is not particularly harmful to cats, but there is great danger in possible transmission to human beings. A pregnant woman exposed to toxoplasmosis risks great danger to her fetus. The disease is transmitted through oocysts in cat feces. Although the chances of infection are slim, pregnant women should avoid contact with litter boxes and care should be taken when gardening, as cats often use the soft soil for elimination.

Coccidiosis is more common in young kittens that in adult cats. It is transmitted from cat to cat via oocysts in the feces. Affected cats may appear weak and will exhibit diarrhea, which may contain blood or mucus. Kaopectate may relieve the diarrhea and prevent dehydration. Severe cases of diarrhea or cats that become anemic may require hospitalization for replenishment of fluids. Carriers of coccidia should be isolated and treated with sulfonamides. The cat's living quarters should be thoroughly disinfected. Antibiotics or sulfa drugs may eliminate this parasite.

Roundworms are usually not life-threatening unless the infestation is so severe that intestinal blockage occurs. These worms can lie dormant in a female cat and be transmitted to her kittens prior to birth. Vomiting, diarrhea and mucus in the stool may indicate roundworms. Fecal exams can reveal their presence; otherwise they may go undetected. Affected cats should be dewormed with medication from your veterinarian.

Hookworms cause anemia due to blood loss. Black or bloody stools may appear in affected kittens. Deworming is the recommended treatment. Hookworms are usually limited to areas with hot, humid climates.

Tapeworms are not usually life-threatening to cats. These commonly found worms are carried by fleas and rodents. When the cat ingests the flea hosts, the tapeworms (and their eggs) are also swallowed by the cat, continuing the life cycle of the tapeworm. Your veterinarian can administer effective medication to rid the cat of worms, but you must eliminate the fleas or the tapeworm will quickly return.

Heartworms are more common in dogs than in cats. However, cats who are exposed to mosquitoes may be in danger (primarily in the southeastern United States). Your veterinarian can test your cat for the presence of heartworm and prescribe preventive medication when risk warrants treatment.

RINGWORM

Ringworm is actually a fungus, not a parasite. Invisible to the naked eye, this infection may be transmitted from animal to animal (including humans). Infected animals can infect others by direct contact (skin to skin) or by indirect contact, as ringworm can be transmitted via spores in the air, contact with objects like grooming tools, or from the soil.

Ringworm usually appears as hair loss and patches of itchy, scaly skin. However, some cats show no signs at all. Infected cats must be treated with veterinary-prescribed medications, including special shampoos for cleaning the infected areas, topical ointments and oral medications.

All pets that have been exposed to an infected animal should be thoroughly examined by a veterinarian. Any items that have had contact with infected animals should be disinfected with diluted bleach or discarded.

MEDICATIONS

Giving medication to a cat can be one of the most challenging aspects of pet ownership. If your veterinarian prescribes a drug for your cat, he or she should demonstrate how to administer it. Unlike dogs, cats will not often fall for the "pill wrapped in a treat" trick. A cat's keen sense of smell will detect the offensive presence of the unwanted substance. Often force is needed to pill a cat.

You must first restrain the cat before you can treat it. Securely wrapping the cat in a towel will allow you access to the cat's mouth without experiencing the wrath of its claws. Some cats are able to over-

36

come the towel trick, which means you must be creative and tough to provide your cat with the medication it needs.

To restrain a struggling cat, firmly grasp the skin on the back of its neck, slightly above the shoulder blades. As the cat struggles, point it away from you and let it tire itself. When the cat settles down, gently but firmly open the cat's mouth and insert the pill or liquid.

Once the medication is in the cat's mouth, be sure it is placed over the tongue and in the back of the throat. Keep the cat's mouth closed and gently and slowly stroke the cat's throat until it swallows. Continue to observe the cat for several minutes, until the medication is ingested. Often your efforts to administer medication are quickly overturned by a vomiting or clever cat. Keep the cat on your lap for a while and pet it. You can distract the cat from its frustrations with the medicating process while you share affection with it.

Your veterinarian will be the person to administer inoculations to your cat, except on the rare occasion that the cat develops a disease (such as diabetes) that requires at-home injections. In such cases, your veterinarian will instruct you in the procedure for giving injections to cats.

Never give over-the-counter medications to your cat without consulting your veterinarian. Seemingly harmless medications can be lethal when given to a cat.

WHEN TO VISIT THE VETERINARIAN

Your cat should receive a yearly examination by a licensed veterinarian. Kittens must undergo a series of inoculations, which will require several trips to the animal hospital. Unless your cat is ill, an annual visit for booster shots, fecal exam and veterinary check-up is all that is required for health insurance. However, you should recognize the danger signs that signal your cat's need for veterinary attention. If your cat displays any of the following signs, call your veterinarian for advice or to schedule an appointment.

Fever (more than 103° F)
Lumps (hard, soft or fluctuant [fluid filled])
Weight changes (unusual)
Change in eating or drinking habits
Head shaking
Sensitivity to touch, or obvious pain

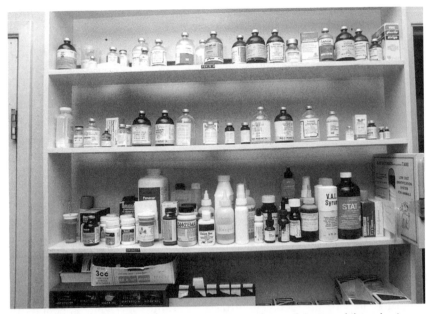

Today's veterinarian has the advantage of a wide spectrum of drugs and therapies to provide better health care for your pet. The wise, caring cat owner takes full advantage of what modern science can do for the quality of feline life.   *Scott McKiernan*

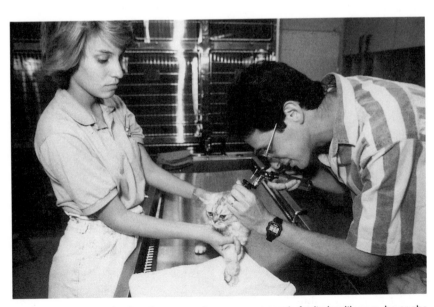

Just as your veterinarian has the preparations your cat needs for its health care, he or she has the skill and diagnostic tools to recognize and deal with any illness even before it becomes evident to the lay observer.   *Scott McKiernan*

Bloated stomach
Bad breath
Vomiting
Diarrhea
Straining to pass stools or urine
Coughing
Breathing difficulties
Discharge from nose, mouth or ears
Pale gums or eye rims
Listlessness or lack of energy

VACCINES

Consult your veterinarian to schedule vaccines for your cat. The previous owner or the animal shelter may provide a history of vaccinations that have been administered to your new cat or kitten.

Adult cats with unknown vaccination histories are usually treated on the same schedule as kittens.

FVR-CP (Feline Viral Rhinotracheitis, Calicivirus, Panleukopenia, or Feline Distemper)

- Kittens are vaccinated at eight, twelve, and sixteen weeks of age.
- Annual boosters follow the kitten shots.
- If an adult cat has no vaccine history, two shots are given one month apart.

Pneumonitis

- Kittens are vaccinated at nine and twelve weeks.
- Annual boosters follow kitten shots.

Leukemia Vaccines

- Feline leukemia vaccine is given at nine weeks of age (or older), a second dose is given one month later.
- Annual boosters follow kitten shots.

Feline Infectious Peritonitis

- Kittens are vaccinated at sixteen and twenty weeks.

- Adult cats receive two vaccines, one month apart.
- Annual boosters follow initial shots.

Rabies

- Kittens are vaccinated once after three months of age.
- Periodic boosters are given—consult your veterinarian for schedules for boosters.
- Cats who spend time out of doors should always be protected from rabies.

As research into feline diseases continues, other diseases may be prevented via vaccination. Be sure to consult your veterinarian for scientific updates.

EMERGENCIES

The best way to treat emergencies is to prevent them. Confining your cat to the indoors and cat-proofing your home can prevent tragedies from happening. But even the most conscientious of cat owners must be prepared to offer first aid to the cat whose curiosity gets it into trouble. At-home first aid is not a substitute for veterinary care; it is a means for sustaining the cat while you make arrangements to have it seen by your vet or by the local emergency clinic. If the need arises, follow these procedures and immediately call your veterinarian for further instructions.

Wounds are often caused by bites from other animals and most often are suffered by cats that roam outdoors. However, cats in multipet households occasionally suffer the teeth of their housemates. Dog bites are usually characterized by tearing of the skin, while cat bites most often produce puncture wounds.

Other wounds are suffered by curious cats who fall on sharp objects or brush against sharp surfaces. You can clean minor wounds with hydrogen peroxide, but more severe injuries require that the veterinarian clean the injured area. Sutures may be required. Antibiotics may be prescribed if the veterinarian suspects infection.

If the wound is bleeding, you must stop the blood flow as soon as possible. Wrap the wound with gauze bandages or strips of toweling. If necessary, apply pressure to the wound to slow the blood flow. Secure the bandage by wrapping strips of cloth around the cat's body, leg, head

The lucky pet that has been neutered and is not allowed outdoors can enjoy seeing the world go by and never be at risk due to accident or injury.   *Nancy Klein*

or tail and tie tightly. If the cat is uncooperative, two people may be needed to complete the task.

Burns should immediately be rinsed with cold water to prevent tissue damage. A cat's stroll across the stove or contact with boiling water or certain chemicals will cause burns. Your veterinarian will determine the degree of severity and treat the area with antibiotics to prevent infection. Severe burns can cause shock—in these cases treat the shock first and the burn afterward.

Choking is characterized by a cat that paws at its mouth, gags and drools. If you notice these signs, hold the cat upside down and press its chest to release the lodged object. Tweezers or needle-nosed pliers can be used to dislodge difficult objects. Surgery is sometimes necessary to remove swallowed objects. Be careful to avoid being bitten while treating choking victims.

Poisoning is seen less often in cats than in dogs. Cats are particular about what they eat, but their fastidious grooming can get them into trouble. A cat that cleans itself ingests the substances that pollute the coat. Substances like antifreeze and insecticides can be ingested by cats as they lick their coats or paws.

Immediately contact your veterinarian or your local poison control center for instructions for treating a poisoned cat. Be sure to identify the source of the poisoning and have a container label nearby if possible. Take the bottle and label with you to the veterinarian. Be prepared for the cat to go into shock, and if this happens, treat accordingly.

Shock can be caused by trauma, poisoning, electrocution or injury. A cat in shock will become cold to the touch; breathe shallow, quick breaths; have a fast but weak pulse and dilated pupils. While you rush a cat in shock to the nearest veterinarian, keep it warm by wrapping it in a blanket and help the blood reach the brain by lowering its head slightly.

If you suspect internal injuries, gently move the cat with one hand supporting the chest and the other supporting the hips. Avoid twisting the cat, and use a blanket or box for a stretcher. CPR (coronary pulmonary resuscitation) is a last-ditch effort to save a failing cat. If your cat is not breathing, or if its heart stops, follow these steps and then get the cat to a veterinarian as soon as possible.

Clear liquid from the cat's lungs by swinging the cat by its hind legs. Or pull out the cat's tongue and press down firmly and quickly on the cat's chest with the palm of your hand. Release quickly to allow air to enter the lungs.

After you have cleared the cat's lungs, hold its mouth closed. Place your mouth over the cat's nose and mouth and blow into the mouth. Let the cat exhale, wait a few seconds and repeat until the cat begins to breathe on its own. If the heart does not beat, lay the cat on its side and pump (with your palm behind the elbow) firmly, approximately one beat per second, while you continue to supply air to the cat's lungs.

These procedures require skill and a calm head. If performed incorrectly they can cause further injury to the cat. Ask your veterinarian to demonstrate these procedures during your cat's next checkup.

The First-Aid Kit

The responsible cat owner is always prepared. In the event of an emergency, you will not have time to gather supplies. Use any convenient, small box to store the things you'll need in an emergency.

Phone numbers: Your veterinarian, the closest emergency veterinary clinic and the poison control center

Bandages: Cotton, gauze, tape and scissors

Tweezers and needle-nosed pliers

Hydrogen peroxide

Antiseptic lotions

Rectal thermometer (a cat's normal temperature is 100° F to 102° F)

Petroleum jelly

Cotton balls or swabs

A muzzle or strips of cotton to restrain a biting (and confused) cat

Towels

Splints

Medications your veterinarian may have prescribed for emergencies (never administer medications to cats without the direction of a veterinarian)

Checklist of Poisonous Plants

Amaryllis bulbs	Jessamine berries*
Angel trumpet	Jimsonweed*
Apricot pits	Larkspur*
Azalea	Laurels
Black walnut hulls	Lily of the valley

*Most toxic.

If your cat can get near enough to your house plants to eat parts of them, be very sure that they are not harmful. Many owners find hanging pots for potentially poisonous plants to be the best means of coexistence between flora and feline fauna.   *Nancy Klein*

When you decide to enjoy the pleasure of a cat's companionship, you also assume complete responsibility for its every health need.

Nancy Klein

Blue morning glory
Castor bean plant*
Climbing lily
Common nightshade berries*
Daffodil bulbs*
Dieffenbachia*
Elderberries
Elephant ears
English ivy*
English walnut hulls
Foxglove*
Hydrangea
Iris bulbs
Jack-in-the-pulpit
Japanese yew berries*

Mistletoe
Narcissus bulbs*
Oleander*
Philodendron
Poinciana
Poinsettia
Poison hemlock*
Poppy
Rhododendron
Rhubarb leaves
Toadstool
Tobacco
Water hemlock*
Yewberries

*Most toxic.

Approximately 60 million cats live in 30 million households in the United States.

5

Just Too Many Cats— Why Spay and Neuter

ON A RECENT visit to my childhood friend Rosie, I was surprised to see that Rosie was the doting owner of a lovely cat—and her seven kittens. When I suggested that she spay the cat, Rosie protested, ''I love the kittens, and if I can't find homes for them they can live on the farm nearby.'' Rosie truly loved the cats, but her naive outlook toward the kittens' futures was shocking. She really believed that the kittens could be happy on the farm. She failed to realize that the farmer didn't really want more cats—he wasn't willing to spend several hundred dollars each year for vaccinations or commit to routine veterinary care. He didn't even want the expense of cat food.

Thousands of naive people fail to spay and neuter their cats each year, resulting in overfilled animal shelters across the country. Kittens are warm, cuddly and cute, but they grow into cats who have needs. There are just too many cats in this world and not enough good homes to send them to. With the cat overpopulation problem, there is simply no reason to bring unwanted lives into this world.

The kindest thing you can do for your adopted cat is to have it spayed (if it is female) or neutered (if it is male). Although your pet may be the love of your life and the envy of all your friends, it is unnecessary for your cat to reproduce to be fulfilled.

Cats do not need to mate to be fulfilled. Your altered pet will be completely content to bring you pleasure. You might want two cats for the company of each other. Have both cats altered and your enjoyment of pet ownership will be doubled.

Nancy Klein

Removal of a cat's ovaries (ovariohysterectomy) and uterus is commonly called spaying. This simple operation is performed by a veterinarian at an animal hospital. Most veterinarians recommend performing this operation when the cat is at least six months of age, but advances in veterinary medicine have resulted in making this procedure safe for kittens as young as two months of age. Shelters are sometimes able to spay cats *before* they leave for their new homes.

In addition to ethical reasons, spaying a cat provides health benefits. You can prevent pyometra, ovarian cysts, tumors, mammary gland disorders, many cancers and some skin disorders by spaying a cat. This operation can also add years to the life of your cat.

There are also behavioral reasons to spay your cat. Intact cats produce pheromones, or scent signals. The female's scent attracts tomcats, who respond by spraying. Marking of territories (with an odorous urine) increases, and savage battles for territories are likely to ensue, injuring cats and destroying property.

Queens (female cats) in heat attract males and demand constant attention. They often become nervous, restless and destructive. Cats in heat do not make good companions.

Castration of male cats (sometimes called neutering) is ethical and humane. This simple procedure reduces spraying tendencies and aggression, and it lessens the odor in the cat's urine. Neutered cats are less likely to roam, and be hit by cars or exposed to outdoor dangers.

Veterinarians are currently experimenting with an injection that neuters male cats and dogs, which has met with great enthusiasm among researchers. This procedure is currently awaiting FDA approval. Check with your veterinarian for updates about this revolutionary medical advance.

Cats recover quickly from spaying and neutering, and costs are sometimes offset by the animal shelter. Ask shelter personnel about low-cost spay/neuter programs in your area.

Noble cats groom themselves.

Nancy Klein

6

Weekly At-Home Physical Exam and Grooming Routine

NOBLE CATS groom themselves. Cats also groom each other. Cats even groom their human companions as an expression of affection. This endearing trait can be traced to the mother cat licking her very young kittens. Infant kittens are dependent upon the mother's licking to aid them in elimination. In addition to voiding the bladder and bowels, this stroking sensation provides emotional stimulation and becomes associated with contentment.

But don't expect your cat to keep clean and healthy on its own. You must regularly groom your cat. The cat's physical and emotional needs can be met in the time you spend grooming it. You can strengthen your bond with your cat (cats love being brushed and stroked) and you can perform a physical examination of your cat during each grooming session.

KEEP IN TOUCH

Your cat depends on you for many of its physical needs. Your attention to your cat's general well-being will contribute to your cat's length and quality of life. Each day set aside some quiet time to spend with your cat, and once each week thoroughly examine the cat and attend to all its grooming requirements.

Provide a stable, nonslip surface for the cat to rest upon during the procedure. A grooming table is a wise investment that will help keep your cat secure and keep your back from tiring during lengthy sessions or when you attend to more than one cat. Such a table can be placed in a grooming area in your home, or you can fold the table for easy storage. This item is available at your local pet-supply store, or via a pet-supply catalog.

Your grooming area should have good lighting and access to an electrical outlet and be quiet and relaxing.

Start at the Top

Begin your routine by focusing on your cat's head. Check inside the ears. Are inner ears healthy and pink, or are they bright red and inflamed? Do the ears appear hot, or do they give off unpleasant odors? Contact your veterinarian promptly if you discover irregular conditions in your cat's ears.

The presence of black, waxy material in the ears may indicate mites. You must clean the ears with a cotton swab and apply medication to get rid of these parasites. Medication is available at pet-supply stores, but it may be wise to consult a veterinarian for assistance in fighting this problem. Mites are highly communicable. If mites are discovered in your cat, all household pets—cats and dogs—should be examined, and treated if necessary.

Cats' eyes are their most alluring feature—the mirror of their personalities. The cat's eyes reflect its origin as a predator. Always alert, focused upon prey, sometimes friendly, sometimes reserved, a cat's glance tells a story. Use your cat's eyes as a monitor of its feelings—emotional and physical.

Examine your cat's eyes and nose. Do they appear bright and shiny? Do you notice a discharge? Does the nose have a discharge? A cat's nose can be damp, but unusual discharges should be reported to the veterinarian.

Open your cat's mouth. Check the cat's teeth and gums. Is the mouth healthy, or do you notice lesions, lumps or bumps? Are the teeth clean, or has tartar accumulated along the gum line? Is the breath fresh, or does an odor turn you away? Learn the normal color of your cat's gums. Pale gum color can indicate anemia or be the first sign of other

Your cat's teeth need occasional attention and tartar removal to remain healthy.

treatable systemic diseases. Schedule a checkup by your veterinarian if you detect any abnormalities.

Does your cat have all its teeth? Kittens normally have twenty-six teeth, while adult cats have thirty. You can help your cat's mouth stay clean by rubbing down the teeth and gums with an abrasive, wet towel. This will help prevent tartar from forming, but every cat needs to have its teeth cleaned occasionally. Removal of tartar protects the teeth and gums, prevents infections from occurring and contributes to your cat's overall good health.

COAT AND SKIN CARE

Before brushing your cat, run your hands over its head, neck, body and extremities. Feel for lumps, bumps, lesions and sores. Discovery of any irregularities gives you an opportunity to treat them—before the condition worsens.

Continue to examine the cat's skin as you begin brushing. Part the coat to the skin, and brush or comb in layers. Look for scratches, parasites, flea dirt, embedded thorns or redness. Be sure to check those hard-to-reach areas—the belly, between paw pads and under the legs.

Brush your cat to remove dead hair. Use a slicker brush on long-haired cats, a bristle brush on short-haired cats. My cats love the massage effect of a curry brush, a rubber bar-shaped brush with bumps that have a soothing effect. Comb through the coat with a fine-tooth metal comb to detect fleas.

Brush out any tangles or mats by securing the hair at the base of the follicle and gently brushing the hair at the tips. As tangles loosen, venture toward the skin until the tangles are dislodged. Try using detangling sprays and lotions, which are available at many pet-supply outlets.

Long-haired cats are particularly prone to hairball formation. When cats groom themselves, they ingest a great deal of hair. This hair accumulation in the intestines causes the cats discomfort. Commercial hairball remedies (like Petromalt) or a few licks of butter can help the cat to expel harmful hair accumulation in the stomach. Cats can usually dislodge hairballs by vomiting, but severe accumulations may require surgical removal. You can prevent the trauma of hairballs by grooming your cats daily—especially during shedding season. Commercial laxatives are specially made to assist cats in expelling hairballs. Most pet-supply outlets

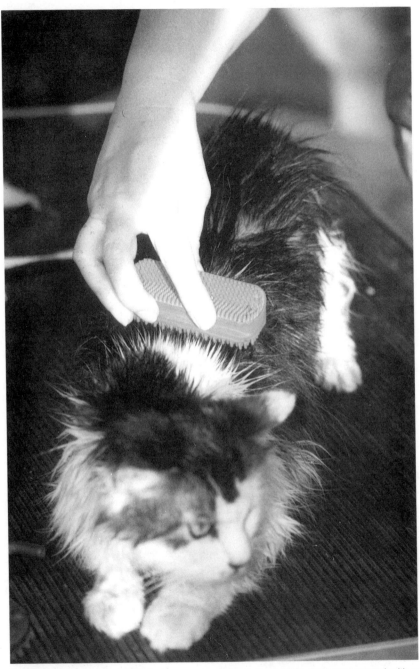

Cats love to be brushed. This is Percy, one of the author's pets, being massaged with a rubber curry brush following his bath.

stock tubes of the laxatives, which owners of long-haired cats should keep on hand.

CARING FOR CLAWS

If your cat's claws become long and very pointed, trim the tips with nail clippers. (Clippers made for humans work just fine.) To trim the claw, begin by pressing gently on the paw pad, and the claw should protrude. Steady the paw and snip off the tip of the nail—be sure to avoid cutting the pink area of the nail, which is a blood vessel. Clip all the claws, including the dewclaws, which are on the insides of the feet, slightly higher than the other claws.

Often cats care for their own nails and don't need human intervention. Scratching posts or climbing activities help to wear down the nails. However, if your cat's claws continually catch in the scratching post, help out and trim its nails.

FIGHTING FLEAS

Pest control is among the greatest challenges to pet owners. Fleas inhabit the United States in staggering profusion and present constant threats to our pets and ourselves. Continual itching follows the bite of a flea, but more serious consequences can develop from flea infestation. Allergic cats may require medication to recover from flea bites, and severely affected individuals can become anemic because the fleas feed on the host's blood.

Fleas are quickly transmitted among pets, and they inhabit homes and yards. Fleas in the house will also feast upon human blood, causing itchy, burning bite marks. Fleas are a host for tapeworms, and eggs of the worm can be transmitted via the bite of a flea. To eliminate fleas you must treat your pets, your house and your yard *at the same time*.

Cats are sensitive to many flea products. BE SURE TO READ THE LABEL OF ANY PESTICIDE YOU USE ON OR NEAR CATS. Some products that are safe for use on dogs are lethal when used on cats. Be certain that the products you use are made especially for cats.

The most effective way to eliminate fleas on a pet is to bathe or dip the pet with flea-killing products. Your cat is likely to fight being immersed in water, so you must be firm and nimble to complete this task quickly.

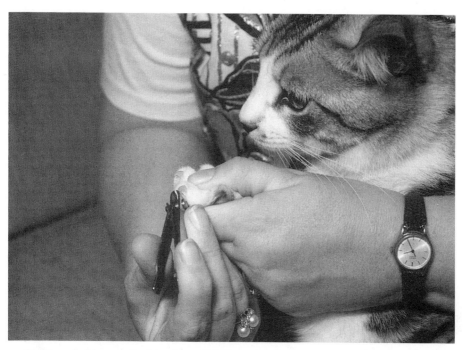

Cutting nails is one part of good grooming that also benefits the household environment. This work should be done in a good light and care should be taken not to cut into the blood vessel, as profuse bleeding and pain will result.

Use a good-quality flea shampoo for your cat's bath and make sure the product is safe for use on cats. Work up a good lather, but be sure to protect eyes and ears.

Thoroughly rinse the soap residue from your cat's coat until the water runs clear. Tense cats will usually relax in the bath once they overcome their fear of the process.

Have several thick terry towels ready before you begin the cat's bath. Although many cats object to being bathed, most love being wrapped in a towel and rubbed dry.

Be sure your cat is thoroughly brushed before bathing it. Mats or tangles worsen when wet. Collect your towels and supplies before you collect your cat.

A cat that struggles can be restrained by putting a harness-type collar on it and attaching a leash. Tie the leash to the spigot, and stand back if the cat's claws appear. Cats have been known to scratch or bite in efforts to avoid a bath. Remain calm, and when the cat relaxes, slowly pour water over the cat's back. You will find the cat eventually relaxes, but don't let your guard down. The cat could spook and thrash at your unprotected arms.

Fleas spend very little time on pets themselves. Fleas live in carpet, dirt and grass, visiting your pets for a meal. Hire an extermination service, or spray the yard and flea bomb the house. If you object to chemical treatments inside the house, try nonchemical products, which are available at some pet-supply stores. Sprinkling borax in your carpet can help control fleas. The borax dries up the flea eggs before they hatch.

People who live in warm climates fight a constant battle against fleas. However, those who live in climates that experience freezing temperatures get relief when the mercury drops.

LOVING IT

Regular grooming sessions will keep your cat healthy and happy. In fact, my cat Ryan loves being brushed so much that I keep her out of the room when I'm grooming other pets. Ryan jumps on the grooming table when she sees anyone being groomed, and she nudges forward to make contact with the brush—she isn't much of a democrat!

Feline curiosity is proverbial. Cats are normally inquisitive and will investigate anything and everything that takes their interest.
Nancy Klein

7

Understanding Your Cat's Behavior

CAT COMMUNICATION is complex and fascinating. In spite of their reputation for independence, cats are very social animals. Cats' interactions with other cats, pets and people help to establish a hierarchy of authority in the home. Cats will claim territories to rule. A favorite chair, a loft in the garage or the landing on the staircase may be claimed by your cat and protected from intruders. Your cat's favorite spots may change periodically, but cats are intent upon protecting what is "theirs."

Before my son, Matt, was born we gathered lots of new things. A crib, a bassinet, a stroller and a playpen were among our acquisitions. Our cat, Percy, delighted in the arrival of each item. For two weeks Percy slept in the bassinet; our protests were to no avail. Then the stroller became Percy's hangout. Playpen, baby swing and nursery furniture each were temporary favorites until Percy tired of them and went back to the front window ledge for his naps.

A casual observer might have concluded that the cat was jealous of the baby-to-be. However, there is nothing unusual about Percy's behavior; he was just being a cat. We let him have his due, washed and disinfected the items, and went on with our lives.

SOUNDS AND SILENCE

Why do cats purr? This endearing behavior is distinctive to domestic cats, whereas wild cats can growl and roar but not purr. Purring is thought to be a sign of contentment and an expression of pleasure. Enjoy the enthusiasm of your purring pet. Get to know your cat's likes and dislikes and look for behavior patterns to determine the significance of your cat's vocalizations.

Many cat owners claim their cats talk to them. While the skeptic may raise an eyebrow, cats really can "talk." Cats vary their meows to have different meanings. One pitch may mean, "I'm hungry," and another can convey, "Pet me, please."

Some sounds have specific meanings. A cat in heat has a distinctive cry. Cats in combat hiss, spit and growl at their opponents. Cats can even talk back to their owners when they disagree with a decision the owner has made.

You don't need to be Dr. Dolittle to talk to animals, but you must be alert, sensitive and observant. The better you develop your communication skills, the more you'll enjoy your pets.

LISTEN TO THE EARS

Your cat's ears can also serve as a mood barometer. Upright, perky ears are the signs of a contented cat. A frightened cat will hold its ears against its head. A cautious cat will fold the ears back while it assesses its immediate situation. Study your cat's ear position and observe what evokes various responses.

TAIL WAGGING

Both cats and dogs wag their tails. Usually a cat's wagging tail is a sign of agitation. Cats in a state of conflict wag the tail in a deliberate manner. The tail is fully fluffed out, arched and flicked from side to side. When your cat displays this behavior, try to identify the cause of the stress and end the conflict as soon as possible.

A secure cat carries its tail straight up, signifying its confidence and contentment.

You don't need to be Dr. Dolittle to talk to animals. . . .

Nancy Klein

FABRIC TEARING

One of the most common reasons given for getting rid of a cat is destruction of household items, especially furniture. Shredded sofas, ruined carpets and threadbare chairs are evidence of neglect in providing a suitable scratching area for the cat.

Simply scolding a cat will not prevent the cat from continuing this behavior. All cats need to scratch. You can, however, redirect your cat's scratching to an appropriate location—a scratching post or toy.

Cats tear at fabric for a variety of reasons, including sharpening of claws to remove old claw sheaths on front claws, for mental relaxation and for exercise. Cats have scent glands on the undersides of their feet, which enable them to scent-mark the fabrics they shred. Thus, scratching also contributes to the marking of territories.

A scratching post is essential for a cat's emotional well-being. You can direct your cat to its post when scratching behavior is exhibited. Catnip can help to attract the cat to this prime location, or the scent of an old garment can lure a cat to its scratching post.

Although many cat owners opt for surgical removal of the front claws, the practice of declawing is frowned upon. This procedure can be physically and emotionally stressful.

GREETINGS

Rolling on the back is a submissive behavior—a friendly greeting usually given only to family members and close personal friends. A cat that rolls on its back lets loose its self-protective instincts and is vulnerable. This simple gesture is the supreme compliment—exhibiting the cat's undeniable trust.

More dominant cats will actively greet their friends. Rubbing against a leg—back and forth, back and forth—allows the cat to exchange scents with the approaching person or pet. This behavior relaxes the cat and is usually followed by paw licking (enabling the cat to enjoy its newly collected scents).

HOPPING

Cats often hop on their hind legs. This behavior is often seen among cats when they greet each other. This friendly gesture is usually followed

Rolling on its back is a friendly greeting a cat usually gives only to family members and close personal friends.

Nancy Klein

Does your cat knead your lap with its front paws?
Nancy Klein

by harmless wrestling and rolling on the ground. Face-to-face rubbing, simulating the strokes a mother cat gives to her kittens, reaffirms cats' affections for each other.

KNEADING

Does your cat knead your lap with its front paws? This slow, deliberate motion is kittenlike and a compliment to you. Secure cats exhibit this behavior with people they trust. Kneading reminds cats of the warmth they experienced as nursing kittens. The kneading that once brought about the flow of mother's milk symbolizes contentment in the adult cat. Often people are bothered by this behavior, not knowing why their cats are messing up their clothing. Cats become confused when owners reject the kneading ritual. If your cat needs to knead, try laying a towel on your lap to provide a suitable surface for those kitty claws.

TERRITORIAL MARKING

Cats, like dogs, mark territories with feces and urine. Tomcats spray continuously to establish their domain. Neutering a tom will help to eliminate this annoying behavior (and will help control the cat population problem). Toms spray the urine as a dominant gesture, inviting challenges from other dominant cats. Fighting among cats often occurs when they return to the spots they have marked.

Outdoor cats should be neutered for their own protection. Indoor cats will curb their tendencies to mark furniture, woodwork and household items if they are neutered.

Submissive cats will bury their feces in an attempt to avoid challenging the dominant members of the species. Submissive and neutered cats rarely have the house-soiling habits seen in dominant intact cats.

SELF-GROOMING

Cats groom themselves to keep clean, but the significance of this behavior has many levels. Dominant cats often groom lesser-ranking cats, licking them behind the ears. Grooming also smooths the fur, providing insulation from temperature extremes.

Grooming is a wonderful stress reliever. The activity occupies their

Many of your cat's physical and emotional needs can be fully satisfied by regular grooming sessions.

Nancy Klein

time and makes cats feel productive. Although this behavior is soothing, the production of hairballs can cause distress for the cat. Cats often regurgitate wads of hair following consumption of their own fur.

Owners should be especially attentive to their cats during shedding seasons—usually spring or early summer—and strip as much hair as possible from their cats. Thorough brushing will remove dead hairs, and prevent ingestion of large quantities of loose hair.

8

Training Essentials

I NEVER met a cat I didn't like; but I have met several that I wouldn't like to live with. In order to share my environment, my cats had to learn some rules. Shredding furniture is not acceptable. Litter boxes have a purpose. Walking on the countertop is banned. Although cats don't require much training, they do require some behavioral modification.

LITTER-BOX TRAINING

Often kittens are introduced to the litter box by their mothers. Mom will nudge the kittens to the box and "instruct" them by stroking the kittens until they urinate and defecate. Mother's attention and physical contact is reward enough to inspire the kittens to return to that area whenever they need to.

Many adult cats need only to learn where a new home's litter box is, and they respond appropriately. Other cats need help in developing acceptable personal habits. If you are unsure of your new cat's habits you must begin conservatively and confine the cat to a safe area (such as a bathroom or laundry room) while the cat demonstrates its litter-box prowess. When the cat consistently uses its box, give the cat more freedom, but observe its behaviors pattern for a few days.

Many adult cats need only to be shown where the litter box is kept in a new home and they will respond appropriately and flawlessly.

Nancy Klein

Shelter personnel hear stories every day of cats who refuse to use the litter box. The most common cause of this problem behavior is the cat's dislike of the litter used. If your cat dislikes its box, experiment with the various litters on the market. These products differ in texture, absorbency and odor, and cats have their preferences. Increasing the frequency of litter changes can also overcome a cat's reluctance to use its box.

Placement of the litter box is important. Put the box in a quiet, accessible area of your house. The garage, basement or bathroom are all possible locations.

Cats may occasionally chose inappropriate areas for elimination but they can be trained to use a designated spot. For example, if your cat heads for a particular room each time it needs to eliminate and you prefer the box to be kept elsewhere, gradually condition your cat to report to the intended area. Begin by placing the box where the cat wants to go. Each day move the box a few feet toward *your* chosen spot. Eventually the cat will follow your lead and utilize the litter box in its desired location.

If your cat seems to prefer inappropriate surfaces for elimination (such as a newspaper, a carpet or towels), lure the cat to its litter box with its object of choice. Place the item (which will later be discarded) in the bottom of the litter box and top it with a small amout of litter. Show the box to the cat and encourage him or her to use it. Each day, change the proportion of litter to the chosen item—reduce the size of the carpet, newspaper or towel and increase the litter amount until the lure is entirely eliminated from the litter box, and the cat willingly uses the litter.

Multicat households often confront litter-box problems. While some cats willingly share their boxes, other refuse to use another cat's toilet. Providing additional boxes usually solves the problem, especially when the boxes are placed in different areas of the house.

Occasionally, litter-box problems can be attributed to a physical illness. If your cat strains to eliminate, has runny stools or urinates frequently, consult your veterinarian.

SCRATCHING POSTS

Cats need a place to stretch and exercise. Simply correcting the cat for clawing at furniture, carpets and drapes is unfair unless you provide an appropriate place for the cat to "work out." You must provide a scratching post, tree or other object to keep your cat content and healthy.

A scratching post, thick branch or similar object is required by every cat to keep its claws in good shape and as a means to encourage play and exercise. *Nancy Klein*

Leash-trained cats are easier to transport to the veterinarian, as they look forward to outings with their people.
Nancy Klein

Purchase or construct a scratching post for your cat. Pet-supply stores and catalogs stock a wide variety of cleverly designed scratching toys. Some reach the ceiling and have many levels for your cat to explore. Others come in designer colors to match your interior decor. Some scratching toys are shaped like mice, cars and mushrooms. A scratching post need not be an eyesore; it can even be a conversation piece.

Handy people can custom-design and build scratching posts using wood, carpet, bark or coiled rope. If you choose to build your cat's claw-catcher, don't use upholstery materials because it may confuse your feline friend.

Pet professionals debate the practice of declawing cats. This procedure is not necessary for the health of the cat but is performed merely for the convenience of the cat owner. During this procedure the end bond that houses the claw is amputated from the cat's front feet. Humanitarians object to the practice and suggest that owners provide ample scratching posts for their cats to enjoy instead.

"Fake fingernails" are available for cats with clawing problems. Plastic nail covers, which prevent the cat from shredding upholstery and furniture, can be secured over the cat's nails. If your cat persists in inappropriate scratching, ask your veterinarian about this product.

WALKING A CAT ON A LEASH

Even indoor cats enjoy an occasional change of scenery. Walking your cat can be enjoyable for you and your cat. Use a leash and harness, and begin with short walks in familiar surroundings. This ritual should begin while your cat is a kitten. Under your supervision let the kitten explore and wander as far as the leash allowed him. You'll enjoy observing its excitement in discovering its environment.

Leash-trained cats are easier to transport to the veterinarian because the cats come to look forward to outings.

CRATE TRAINING

Although crate training is generally recommended for dogs, cats can also benefit from this wonderful device. I keep two sizes of crates for my cats—one for transporting the cats and one for confining them while at home.

Although the cats usually enjoy free run of the house, there are times when the cats must be confined. I have large crates that contain bedding, a small litter box, and food and water dishes for each cat.

To accustom your cat to a crate, place your equipped "den" in a quiet area of your house. Put the cat in the crate with its favorite dinner and let the cat enjoy its meal. Leave the cat in the crate for a half hour the first time. Do not release the cat if it fusses; instead, cover the crate with a blanket (but provide for air circulation). Gradually increase the time you crate until the cat can be confined for several hours at a time.

I feed my cats in crates each evening, to prevent my dogs from consuming the cats' tempting morsels. The crate is especially useful when I need to monitor the food intake of a particular cat. On occasions when guests or your activities make it inconvenient to have the cat roam your house, you can comfortably confine the cat in its crate.

TEACHING "COME"

Many cats learn their names at an early age and will respond to the sound of their names by coming to the caller. Usually the cat's owner has conditioned the cat to respond to the sound of its name by providing (often before a meal) pleasant associations. Always greet your cat with pleasant experiences, and your cat will come to your call enthusiastically.

To speed your cat's response, devote an afternoon to teaching this behavior. Use your cat's natural fondness for hunting to entice it to come to you. As you dangle a piece of ribbon or a kitty toy, call the cat, "Fluffy, come!" As the cat approaches, encourage it with soft expressions: "Good, come." When the cat reaches you, give it a treat and praise it. Repeat this sequence several times until the cat automatically responds to your command. When the cat is consistent, begin eliminating the food reinforcer. Eventually you will need to reward it with food only occasionally.

TEACHING TRICKS

Cats can be taught behaviors in much the same way other animals are taught, using behavior modification. The rules are simple, and you can easily learn what kinds of stimuli make your cat responsive. All training should be positive and fun for you and the cat. Harsh corrections and physical punishments will only discourage a cat.

Begin by selecting a behavior that becomes your cat; for example,

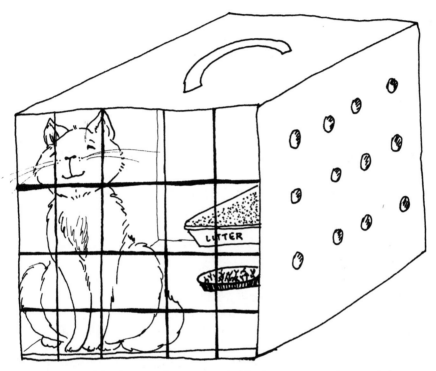

Although crate training is generally recommended for dogs, cats can also benefit from this wonderful approach to pet management. *Nancy Klein*

waving to the crowd. Tell your cat to "wave," while you dangle a piece of string in front of the cat's face. As the cat swats at the string, proclaim "good wave," stop dangling the string, and give the cat a food reward (a food reward should be something extremely pleasing to the cat such as chicken, tuna or cheese). Repeat this sequence for several days, then gradually eliminate the string. Cut the string a few inches at a time until the string is hardly noticed by the cat. After the string is completely eliminated, reduce the frequency of the food rewards. At first you will reward every wave, then every other wave, and eventually the rewards will be few and far between. Use this method to teach tricks you like.

ELIMINATING UNWANTED BEHAVIORS

Just as you can encourage certain behaviors in cats, you can discourage offensive behaviors. The key to ridding your cat of undesirable habits is to appropriately punish the cat while it is *in the act*.

For example, if you want to keep your cat from walking on countertops, you must correct the cat as soon as it jumps upon the surface. You can scold the cat in a harsh voice, clap your hands, or spray the naughty cat with water when it attempts this behavior (try a plant mister or plastic spray bottle).

You can make a rattle can by placing pennies in an empty soda can and taping the top shut. When the cat jumps on the counter, toss the rattle can toward the cat's feet. Your target is not the cat, but the surface near the cat. The noise from the rattling pennies should startle the cat, causing it to leap from the counter.

If you are out of sight or out of the cat's thoughts when you toss the can, the cat will not associate the punishment with your presence. The cat is then less likely to jump on the countertop during your absence.

Some rewards are stronger than some punishments. A cooling roast beef left on a counter is too much temptation for even the best-trained cat. There are times when confining the cat is the practical and humane thing to do.

Be sure that your punishments *are* punishments. If your harshest correction is "Bouncer, you're such a naughty cat," spoken in a soft voice, your cat is unlikely to be adversely affected by your declaration. Punishments must be unpleasant (but humane) to be effective.

Commercial sprays are available to keep cats off anything they shouldn't touch. For the cat that prefers the sofa to its scratching post, cat-repellent sprays can be applied to the sofa target. When the cat approaches the sofa, its first impression will be the unpleasant odor (to the cat) of the spray. The cat is likely to avoid the couch as long as it can detect the odor. Spraying the couch simulates a cat's natural tendency to mark territories.

By spraying the couch you are telling the cat, "This is mine." Most cats will respect your claims, but dominant cats may challenge your supremacy and "spray" the couch themselves. Be present to observe your cat's first encounter with the sprayed couch. If the cat positions itself to spray, immediately correct it with your voice, water, noise or toss a rolled paper in the cat's direction (not to clobber the cat, but to startle it).

Many houseplants are toxic to cats. Teach your cats to avoid your houseplants. If your cat seeks out a particular plant, paint the closest leaves with a mixture of flour, water and chili peppers or hot sauce. The cat who licks a leaf will receive immediate punishment.

Punishments must be immediate and consistent to be effective. A cat can't read your mind. If you decide to keep the cat off a favorite chair, it must *never* be permitted to roost on that spot. Allowing the cat to sit on the chair—except when company is present—will only confuse the cat. Decide upon your rules and stick to them.

Your cat's favorite forms of play approximate the natural behaviors used in hunting.
Nancy Klein

9

It's Playtime!

CATS RELISH PLAY every day. Their favorite forms of play imitate the behaviors they would use in hunting: chasing, stalking, pouncing, batting and juggling. Outdoor cats have more opportunity to fulfill their exercise needs, but indoor cats can become sedentary—usually as a result of becoming bored with their environment.

Although cats spend a great deal of their time sleeping, their up-time is important. After several hours' rest, cats are ready to play. Exercise is important to your cat's physical well-being and vital to its emotional health.

You should provide two types of entertainment for your cat—participatory (games that include you) and nonparticipatory (games your cat can play alone). Participatory games are the most fun. You can share in your cat's fun while forming closer bonds with it.

TEASERS

Boris, a slender Siamese mix, loves to be teased. He'll play for hours with anyone who will dangle a feather from a stick. Sandra, his owner, made Boris's tease toy with a one-yard-long dowel rod, a yard of sturdy string and a few feathers (taken from a feather duster).

Boris expects a friendly tease-match each evening. When Sandra finishes washing her dinner dishes, Boris runs to the closet where the toy is stored. Sandra indulges Boris by dangling the feather a few inches from the ground and bouncing it around the floor.

Boris postures by crouching on the floor, stalking the feather. When Boris feels the time is right, he pounces on his feather target. Sandra often lifts the toy just before it can be ''caught.'' And the game continues.

You can make a toy like Boris's, or purchase one. You will be amazed by the variety of toys available off the shelf or from pet-supply catalogs. Vendors at cat shows tell me that tease toys are their best-selling products.

BATTER UP

Small balls, stuffed mice and rolled paper are victims of cat play each day. No superball is safe in our house when Ryan feels like playing. Often our activities are interrupted when Ryan ''goes to work.'' ''What's that?'' is often answered with the discovery of Ryan knocking into a table leg. This batting game consumes Ryan, making her oblivious to anything in her path.

You should provide battable toys for your cats, but be careful to pick them up when not in use. Small balls can trip people and cause serious injury. Also, be sure that the toys you provide aren't so small or alluring that the cat is liable to swallow them.

CAPTURE GAMES

Cat-toy manufacturers continue to become progressively more creative. All cats love to chase balls, but when the ball's confined the cat will love the chase even more. Meeser loves his ball-trap toy—a Ping-Pong ball trapped inside a round plastic container. The container has a hole on the top for Meeser to spy on the ball and for his paw to fit through. Meeser swipes and paws the rolling ball, but he can never *quite* get it out. I love to watch Meeser's intense expression as he ponders the ball. This toy is available through pet-supply outlets and is sure to win the affection of your cats, too.

A cat can spend hours with its toys. Active playthings are most appreciated, and if they are also catnip scented, the user's pleasure is that much greater.

In the home, cats will invent games and find numerous ways to amuse themselves. If there are two cats in the home, they will happily innovate together.

PLAY FETCH

Cats love to fetch—yes, I'm talking about cats. A favorite toy is the most likely to succeed as a fetching item. My cat Percy fetches cellophane papers. He loves the sound they make when they are crinkled—it will bring him running at any time of day.

I crinkle the paper to get Percy's attention. When he's alert and ready, I toss the cellophane across the room. Percy springs after the paper, batting it in the air until he catches it. Percy proudly delivers his catch to me and impatiently waits for the next toss.

POINT OF VIEW

Cats like to observe their world. Even indoor cats enjoy watching birds, people and other pets through a window. You can place a scratching post, a cat-proof table or a covered chair near an interesting window to satisfy your cat's curiosity. Pet-supply outlets carry window perches to make cats comfortable on the windowsill. These perches firmly attach to a regular window and are covered in scratchable carpet for added enjoyment.

A window seat will quickly become a favorite spot for cat naps.

HERBAL ECSTASY

Catnip is a longtime favorite treat for domestic cats. This herb acts as a stimulant, encouraging playful behavior. Even a lazy cat will come to life after sniffing a pile of catnip. Provide your cat with the pleasure of catnip occasionally. If the cat has constant access to the substance it will lose its effect and may dull the cat's appetite. Purchase loose catnip, sprinkle it on newspaper and watch the cat come alive! Catnip toys are among my cats' favorites. A blue, catnip-filled dinosaur has been "killed" by Ryan a thousand times.

BUILD A CITY

Cats love to explore. Unfortunately, the confines of your home can become boring for your cat—unless you use some creativity. Change your cat's environment by building a city within your four walls. Cardboard boxes can become buildings when a doorway is cut into the structure. Stack empty boxes and build tunnels of boxes and paper bags to amuse your cat. Empty paper bags make wonderful caves and empty toilet paper rolls are fun to hunt down. Toys don't have to be expensive to be fun.

A working cat is a happy cat. Since our cats don't need to fend for themselves, we must provide stimulation for their mental and physical well-being. Your cat's pleasure is limited only by your imagination.

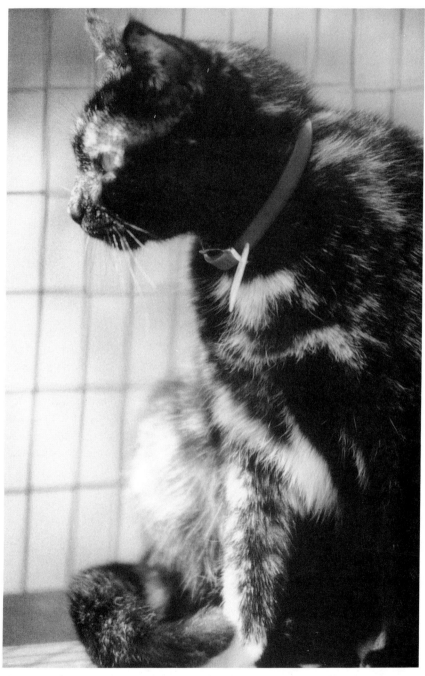

The quality of life that a pet enjoys depends on the compassion and dedication of its owner.

10

Pet Responsibility

***

W HEN PEOPLE arrive at an animal shelter, they are often overwhelmed by the abundance of great-looking pets that are available for adoption. Visions of scraggly strays and vicious, attacking critters are replaced by reality. Millions of healthy, attractive, likable cats and dogs are abandoned by their owners each year. The lucky discards find their way to animal shelters, where dedicated workers strive to find suitable homes for the furry castaways. The unfortunate strays suffer on our streets, scavenging for food, battling disease and starving for affection.

BENEFITS AND OBLIGATIONS

Pet ownership brings a host of benefits. Warmth and companionship, a purring pet and the listening ear of a furry friend are irreplaceable. Pet ownership has been proven to lower blood pressure, improve mental health and maintain balance in one's life. Stories abound of heroic pets that awaken owners to the threat of fire, make parents aware of children in dangerous situations and alert residents to the presence of intruders in the household.

Along with the benefits of pet ownership come serious responsibilities. The quality of life that a pet enjoys depends on the compassion and dedication of its owner. Although individual human life-styles will dictate the life-style of each pet, every self-respecting pet owner must meet minimum standards for rearing pets.

1. An owner must provide for the physical comfort and safety of his or her pets. Pets should have protection from the elements (wind, rain, snow and sunshine) and should be able to escape a storm or retreat from blistering heat.
2. Nutritional needs of pets must be met. Quality food, water—and when necessary—dietary supplements are important to maintain good health.
3. Pet owners must pay for the medical needs of their pets. Vaccinations, yearly veterinary examinations and treatment for injury or disease are basic rights of every pet.
4. No responsible pet owner willingly contributes to pet overpopulation. Pets should be spayed or neutered as early as a veterinarian can perform the procedure. (Responsible breeders curb their breeding activities, taking into account the quality of their breeding stock and their ability for placing puppies and kittens in appropriate homes).
5. Pet owners will provide emotional stimulation for their pets. A bored cat or dog leads a tedious life. Often boredom contributes to physical problems (overweight, sores made by compulsive licking of an area of skin, etc.) and behavior problems.
6. Cats need grooming and a clean environment. Most cats do a good job of grooming themselves, but occasionally help is needed. Weekly brushing is enjoyable for the cat, and will help remove excess dirt and loose hair, as well as prevent hairball formation. An occasional bath may be needed from time to time.
7. Your cat needs exercise. You must provide the stimulation to keep your cat from becoming fat and lazy.
8. Having pets is sometimes a constant battle with parasites. Keeping your cat free of fleas, ticks, worms and lice will improve its health and keep the pests from bothering humans as well.
9. You must protect your pet from suffering.
10. You must provide your cat with love and affection. Appreciation of your cat's beauty and personality will help you enjoy each other for many years.

If you can satisfy the needs of a cat, the benefits of companionship and endless entertainment are yours for a lifetime.

Did you know that:

- Every hour, 2,000 to 3,500 hundred puppies and kittens are born in the United States—more than 30 million each year.
- Only 1 in 10 of these animals will find a permanent home.
- A dog abandoned in the street has a life expectancy of one year; a cat, slightly longer (assuming they're not hit by cars first).
- Only 20 to 25 percent of animals brought to the nation's public pounds and private shelters are adopted. The rest must be destroyed, at an annual cost approaching $400 million.
- If a dog or cat has four offspring every year (a conservative number), two of them female, and each of these females also has four offspring a year, two of them female, by the seventh year, the original mother will have 4,372 descendants!

(Facts furnished by the Pasadena Humane Society and SPCA.)

Percy developed a special relationship with Teddy, the youngest dog. Teddy allowed Percy to grip the thick hair of her mane while she walked around the yard dangling a contented cat.

Nancy Klein

11

Happy Endings

PERCY

Percy was born in a barn. His mother lived off the mice she caught. She never received inoculations. She wasn't spayed. Percy entered the world with an uncertain future.

My sister Becky brought Percy home on impulse. A situation that was doomed to failure somehow worked out because my parents were willing to accept responsibility for the cat. Percy lived six years with my parents and then came to live with my husband and me. As much as I liked Percy, I was apprehensive about bringing him home—after all, I had three dogs who had never been around cats. Would this work out?

Percy was quickly crate-trained to fly cross-country with me. When we arrived in California, Percy stayed in his crate while the dogs investigated the new arrival. Luckily, my dogs (Keeshonds by nature are accepting of most creatures) welcomed Percy into their pack. In fact, Percy developed a special relationship with Teddy, the youngest dog. Teddy allowed Percy to grip the thick hair of her mane while she walked around the yard dangling a contented cat.

Today cats, dogs and my son, Matt, require my time and energy—luckily, they all enjoy each other, which brings me great pleasure.

PERCY — from an uncertain future to the life
of Riley.   *Scott McKiernan*

RYAN — once a sick, abandoned kitten and
now a living testimony to loving kindness

RYAN

The shelter worker told me the little black kitten was found in a trailer park. It appeared that the owners of her mother discarded the entire litter of her kittens at a place where people were likely to find them.

The irresponsible cat owners failed to spay their cat and she, of course, reproduced. Instead of providing for the kittens, they dumped them, leaving someone else to get them to the animal shelter.

The black kitten arrived at the Irvine (California) Animal Care Center with a severe case of ringworm and an ear-mite infestation. Shelter personnel nursed her back to health under the supervision of a generous volunteer veterinarian. Shaving the coat, daily baths, and continuous medical procedures colored the kitten's lengthy shelter stay.

When I saw the special needs of this gangly feline, I knew she needed someone capable of treating her illnesses, so I applied to become her new owner. The shelter insisted on keeping the kitten until the ring-worm had cleared, thus eliminating the threat of spreading the fungus to my other pets.

The black kitten came home needing a name. My young son, Matt, enthusiastically offered to name her Ryan. At first I refused—after all, the cat was female! But somehow the name stuck.

Ryan was promptly spayed and gradually introduced to our family. Matt was instructed to be patient with the new cat. My husband had an allergic reaction to Ryan until I bathed her and soaked her in Allerpet. Ryan was crated for her introduction to Percy and our dogs.

The dogs welcomed Ryan, as I expected. But Percy really surprised me. Since he had been an "only cat" for eight years, I wasn't sure Percy would allow another cat to violate his territory. I anticipated an adjustment period, but Percy immediately accepted the newcomer—perhaps because a kitten posed no threat to Percy's dominance. Today Percy and Ryan are best buddies. They romp and play with zest and glee. I'm sorry I waited so long to get Percy a feline friend.

Ryan has one bad habit I can't seem to break her of—she stretches lengthwise across the width of the bed and forces me to sleep on a corner of the mattress.

FLEA

A young cat was taken to the veterinarian for vaccinations and neutering in June of 1979. The procedures were completed and the pretty

FLEA — purposely abandoned at a caring place

SPICE — owing it all to a dedicated marine

kitty waited and waited for his owners to claim him. When the owners failed to show up, the veterinary staff called the phone number on the admittance forms and discovered that the number had been falsified. Further investigation showed that the address was also fake; obviously, the kitten had been purposely abandoned at a caring place, and he thus joined the ranks of homeless cats.

Luckily for Flea, he was adopted almost immediately. Twelve years later, Flea's owner has happy memories of Flea participating in every important family event. On a cross-country trip from Virginia to California, a leash-restrained Flea was even allowed to frolic through some snow.

Flea's household is happily shared with other pets, but he is "boss cat." He is a rich brown tabby with golden eyes that don't show any signs of age. He has enriched the lives of his family—human, canine and feline members—and he is likely to live a long, full life.

SPICE

USMC Camp Pendleton is a large military base in southern California. Some of the best-trained, physically intimidating military personnel in the world refine their skills under the bright skies of Pendleton. One day, when Paul, a dedicated marine, was due for recertification during the annual rifle competency tests, he spent his lunch hour near the rifle range on the base and noticed a cat surveying the grounds. Asking around, Paul learned that the cat was the resident mouser and that she had a litter of kittens nearby.

Paul looked for the kittens and eventually located them. But he was shocked to discover them undernourished, restless and crying. Paul claimed the motley crew and nursed them back to health. He also had the mother spayed. Through persistence, he managed to find homes for three of the kittens, but struck out trying to place the fourth. The scrawny kitten rode home with Paul on his motorcycle. Tucked inside Paul's leather jacket, the kitten relaxed against his chest. Today Spice and Paul share a special bond, no doubt in appreciation for his honorable actions.

TIGGER

Tigger wandered to the doorstep of Joanne Stout in Huntington Beach, California, several years ago. He was infested with fleas and

TIGGER — thanks to those lucky toes?

SQUIRT — so full of energy she never seemed to rest

drastically underfed, and his shoulders and hipbones showed under the skin. A broken tail and whiskers hinted of past horrors the cat had undergone.

After feeding and defleaing the small cat, Joanne took him to the veterinarian, where he was dewormed and vaccinated. The broken tail had already started to repair itself—although a bit crookedly—so the vet left it alone.

Joanne presented the rejuvenated kitten to her softhearted friends the Palikas. Today Tigger weighs in at a healthy seventeen pounds and attracts attention because of the extra toes on his front feet. In the tradition of New England sailors, Tigger would be considered lucky because of those extra toes. Perhaps there's some truth in that old belief!

TROUBLES

Seated in the middle of a busy freeway, a tiny kitten watched the cars whiz by. A sharp-eyed motorist spotted the furball and (illegally) parked her car on the center divider. Risking a ticket, Liz leaned over a concrete slab and called, "Here Kitty, Kitty . . ." Terrified that the cat would be frightened of her rescuer, Liz very slowly worked her way to the cat. The kitten peeked at Liz, then quickly shut her eyes, as if to close out this overwhelming world.

When Liz reached the kitten, she quickly grabbed the cat by the scruff and hurried back to the car. Safe inside, the kitten went limp, exhausted from her experience. Naming the kitten Troubles, Liz sped home.

The episode has left the kitten emotionally scarred. She is shy and hides from strangers. She dislikes changes in her routine and panics on car rides. She is a very sweet cat, with an adorable chirpy meow. Troubles is well loved—idiosyncrasies and all.

SQUIRT

Squirt was found hanging around the shopping center where Bob worked. Afraid that the kitten would run into traffic, Bob carried her home that night. Unfortunately, Bob and his wife already had five cats, so they presented the new find to Bob's sister, who had only four cats. Squirt, then about six months old, was so full of energy she never seemed to rest.

MOLLY — from the streets to an office and finally to a loving home of her own

DICKENS — a quick study with Kinji, a Siamese perchmate

Luckily, she's an affectionate cat and demanding of quality time. When her human companions are too busy to oblige her demands, Ursa, an Australian Shepherd, provides needed strokes. Squirt rolls under Ursa's head and rubs against the dog's chin. The unlikely pair sleep together, with Squirt curled between Ursa's front paws.

MOLLY

Molly once resided at the editorial offices of Fancy Publications, where she kept everyone in good spirits. Unfortunately, an employee developed severe allergies to her, and the cat was forced to find another home. The search was short-lived because Molly is so charming, and Kathy Shaymon happily volunteered to adopt the office mascot.

Molly has a knack for opening closets and cabinets. Perhaps because she is always on the hunt for a good meal, or just because she is very curious, she enjoys exploring and finding new things in the apartment.

Molly will eat just about anything. Although she's on a very strict diet, she still begs for treats during Kathy's meals. Kathy supplies low-calorie wheat grass, which Molly relishes, and she plays catch with the cat to provide much-needed exercise.

Molly was originally rescued from the streets of Los Angeles to become a contented office cat; but Molly has never been happier than she is now, living in a real home.

DICKENS

After the loss of a cat to FIP, Suzanne wanted another. A local pet store allows a rescue group to display their adoptable cats in front of the store on weekends. There Suzanne spotted a beautiful silver-and-black tabby. It was love at first sight for cat and cat lover.

Dickens loves to make noise, and has learned to rattle Suzanne's miniblinds to get her attention. He is also a great talker. He answers to his name and loves to watch aquarium fish. Dickens also loves cheese-and-pepperoni pizza. Suzanne must guard this delicacy from the bandit cat, but she consoles him by having him play his favorite game—feather chasing.

KIKI

A stray cat wandered to Suzanne's door; the cat was a bundle of skin and bones. She fed the cat for a few weeks, wondering if he belonged to anyone in the neighborhood. After a few weeks of feeding the cat (and no evidence of other ownership) Suzanne brought the stray indoors to join her and her Siamese, Kinji.

Kiki likes to carry around his favorite ball. When the ball is in his mouth, Kiki seems to talk, showing off his prized possession. Kiki is a stable cat and loves to knead Suzanne's lap. He tolerates the other household cats and will do anything for tuna.

MEESER

Knowing her passion for Siamese cats, the vet called Suzanne to tell her about a kitten that had been deserted at his office. Meeser was not long homeless.

Meeser likes to play with cellophane wrappers; the crinkle sound is great. Any toy on a string is sure to hold his attention as well.

Meeser is a kleptomaniac and plays with the things he steals. He once stole a gold-and-sapphire bracelet—luckily, Suzanne knows his favorite hiding places! Meeser enjoys playing with other cats, but Suzanne is his favorite object of affection.

PANDORA

A neighbor found Pandora lying on her front steps and brought her to Kim and Jerry Thornton. She knew they had cats, and she didn't know what else to do with the kitten. Kim accepted the cat saying, "I'm sure I can place her with someone at work." Three years later, Kim and Jerry still have Pandora.

Pandora has a very bold personality, which is at once cute and exasperating. Nothing scares her, and she won't take no for an answer. Kim likes Pandora because she has a loving personality—in spite of her other flaws. Pandora is always willing to give or receive affection.

KIKI — knew which door to come up to

MEESER — a kleptomaniac can also steal hearts

PANDORA — at once cute and exasperating

CARMEN — her name is all
that's left of her wayward past

CARMEN

Barbara and Steve Munk adopted Carmen from a Chicago shelter, where they learned that she'd been a street cat, was eight months old and had just delivered a litter of kittens. The Munks couldn't leave without the sorrowful cat. Music lovers, the Munks named their feline treasure after the famous opera, perhaps because of the cat's previous gypsy life.

The first several months brought out the aggressive side of Carmen's personality, with the Munks' other cat, Whiskers, the target of Carmen's anxieties. However, Whiskers was calm and gentle and happy to have feline companionship, so the situation worked out well.

Eight years after adoption, Carmen is friendly and outgoing. She is not afraid of anything and is very curious about new people. The Munks' son Alex, who is five years old, is Carmen's favorite person. In fact, she treats him like her own child!

". . . a cat can fill an empty room and provide tranquillity where loneliness once unsettled the space."

12

Talking to the Cats Around Us

THE CAT'S ESSENCE has a charming effect on me, although many otherwise sane people become phobic when cats enter their environment. For me, a cat can fill an empty room and provide tranquillity where loneliness once unsettled the space. Without being underfoot, my cats participate in my life. They "supervise" daily activities, perching sink side while I prepare for the beginning of a day and finally dozing through the late-night news; my cats are always there.

While cats seem to analyze my activities, they rarely criticize. Providing them with late dinners (which happens more often than I'd like) is my most distressing sin, according to the cats. Percy shows his displeasure by going directly to the refrigerator and yowling. His pacing by the fridge is mirrored by Ryan, who at a distance of five to six feet marks time with precision footwork, never letting me out of her sight.

Percy is a sweet but vocal pet, while Ryan is excitable and frisky. Their demonstrations of complaint represent their outlooks on life. Percy expects to be waited on; Ryan begs for what she wants. Although cats share many behaviors, individual personalities shine through with each and every cat.

Owners must get to know their cats to develop the cat-to-person communication that is so appreciated by cat lovers. When cats and people share friendship, magic can happen. We read each other's moods. I can coax a cranky cat out of his melancholy with a five-minute massage. Percy can convey that enough work is enough—when he plants his body in front of my computer screen. Attempts to shoo him away are in vain—like a bouncing ball, he's right back. My choices are few; stop work or lock the cat out of the room. Whatever the course of action, Percy is always successful—I always stop and consider my progress, my stress level and the time. Whether I stop or persevere is inconsequential; Percy's reminder that a break is due helps keep me on track.

While visitors to my home see that I have cats, most will just see that they are there. Cats don't display their most wonderful qualities to just anyone. Earning a cat's trust takes time, and cats don't relax around people who pose threats. My special friends have acknowledged that Percy and Ryan are special—as are all cats. These friends have been honored with the cats' displays of affection.

GETTING ACQUAINTED

First impressions are very important in establishing a relationship with a cat. Some cats—like some people—will run up to greet newcomers. Others are immediately suspicious of anything or anyone new to them. Cats display their personalities and should be given the first opportunity to approach an unfamiliar visitor.

Don't overwhelm a cat; aggressive approaches will usually frighten a cat and cause it to retreat. You cannot force a cat to entertain your advances; attempts to restrain a timid cat may cause stress that could take weeks to overcome.

The best way to approach a cat is to first let the cat observe you for a while before you make any friendly overtures. Enter the room and avoid eye contact with the cat. Allow him or her some privacy. Soft noises, cooing and slow movements will accustom the cat to your presence.

As the cat begins to relax, slowly approach, but pay attention to the cat's comfort level as you get closer. A secure but gentle demeanor is best appreciated by felines. When you are within reaching distance, resist the urge to grab or even to stroke the cat. Instead, offer your hand to the cat for examination. Give it a chance to take in your smells and get a closer look at you.

The cat will respond with glances at your face. Often this is an invitation to proceed with the introduction. A scratch under the chin is less aggressive to a cat than petting as most people do it. Begin with a

"Nobody who is not prepared to spoil cats will get from them the rewards they are able to give to those who do spoil them." —Sir Compton MacKenzie, English writer

chin scratch, follow by stroking the head, back and tail. But avoid rubbing the cat's tummy. This gesture is very intimidating to cats and can ruin your progress in bonding. In trying to win a feline friend, keep in mind:

Cats are reserved.
Cats flirt.

Cats are curious.
Cats are indifferent.

Cats sometimes like to be touched.
Cats sometimes hate to be touched.

OUTDOOR TERRITORIES

Sarge sits under a parked car in front of his house. The big tabby rules the road for the length of three houses on his side of the street. Sarge is content, unless another cat dares to set foot on his turf. Then Sarge approaches the intruding feline with a look that warns, "Back off."

Sarge is willing to defend his territory and has clearly marked the boundaries of what he considers his. Urine marking, scratch marking and rubbing against borders have outlined (in cat language) the limits of Sarge's home.

Few felines violate his domain. Intruders are met with physical challenges. Sarge will spit, scream and fight to keep what is his. Luckily, our street is quiet, but in neighborhoods everywhere the Sarges of the world routinely come home with battle scars. Not only are these scratches and bites painful and costly to repair, but the wounds also allow diseases to be transmitted from cat to cat, and infections can develop even in innocent wounds.

Neutering outdoor cats is a must. Sexually intact cats are more likely to vie for territorial dominance. Current vaccinations can prevent the spread of disease, but confining the cat indoors or in an enclosure is the only way to adequately protect your feline pets.

INDOOR TERRITORIES

Cats who share a home must learn to live in harmony. Although most cats are somewhat friendly toward other members of their species, initial meetings usually involve unfriendly moments. Indoor cats establish

Your cat will appreciate having access to the outdoors, but this should be provided in the form of a secure enclosure and made available only to those that have been altered.

Cats can enjoy toys in a variety of ways and the toys need not be expensive to be well used.

Indoor cats will adopt their own territories within the home much as outdoor cats and wild cats will in their own element. It is important for us to be sure that the spaces in our homes devoted to our cats are as safe for them as they can possibly be made.

" . . . make the world a better place for cats—surely, they deserve that much."

territories, although they usually can learn to share their domain. Owners should carefully plan introductions of new pets to old, acknowledging both pets' needs.

Homebound cats may release territorial boundaries and share the house without reservation, or each cat may claim areas for exclusive dominion. Owners should respect their cats' preferences whenever possible. Cats may have long-term claims to certain spots, or they may rotate their preferences. Percy seems to select a "spot of the week" and confine himself to that area. Then, for variety, he'll pick a new perch on Monday. When Ryan approaches the chosen land, a glance from Percy sends Ryan to seek out another resting spot.

SOME THOUGHTS IN CLOSING

Animal overpopulation is, by this time, no novelty, but it continues to be a disgrace. Until every pet owner takes advantage of the opportunity to neuter or spay the family pet, shelters and humane societies will be faced with the sorry burden they continue to shoulder—because *someone has to do it.*

Writing this book has been a very positive experience for me, and I am proud to have done it. If, by reading *Adopting Cats and Kittens,* you have been made more aware of and sensitive to the plight of unwanted animals in our society, I am truly gratified. I hope that it means that you will consider adoption as a means of acquiring a pet and that your pet will never contribute to the pathetic surplus of homeless, unhappy, sick and starving animals currently in our midst.

Admittedly, ours is far from a perfect world, and in such a world, suffering is a fact of life. Unwanted cats are not the only ones suffering in today's society. But maybe, if caring people take in strays—from streets or shelters or wherever—populations of shame will decline. And maybe, if these same people we share the world with act to stem the tide of unsupervised population growth, the cats and other animals we share the world with will be better off. Maybe, if these things come about, we may stop seeing the mangled remains of cats on highways or the signs on trees proclaiming "free kittens."

Love your cats and love all cats and do what you can to make the world a better place for cats—surely, they deserve that much.

" The smallest feline is a masterpiece." —Leonardo Da Vinci

Recommended Reading

Benjamin, Carol Lea. *Second-Hand Dog: How to Turn Yours into a First-Rate Pet*. New York: Howell Book House, 1988.

Carlson, Delbert G., D.V.M., and James M. Giffin, M.D. *Cat Owner's Home Veterinary Handbook*. New York: Howell Book House, 1983.

Fox, Michael W. *Supercat: Raising the Perfect Feline Companion*. New York: Howell Book House, 1991.

Cat Fancy Magazine: The Magazine for Responsible Cat Owners (Fancy Publications, P.O. Box 6040, Mission Viejo, CA 92690). This magazine is published monthly and is widely available on newsstands or by subscription.

Nancy Klein

Nancy Klein